COSMIC THING

Praise for the series:

It was only a matter of time before a clever publisher realized that there is an audience for whom *Exile on Main Street* or *Electric Ladyland* are as significant and worthy of study as *The Catcher in the Rye* or *Middlemarch* . . . The series . . . is freewheeling and eclectic, ranging from minute rock-geek analysis to idiosyncratic personal celebration — *The New York Times Book Review*

Ideal for the rock geek who thinks liner notes just aren't enough — *Rolling Stone*

One of the coolest publishing imprints on the planet — *Bookslut*

These are for the insane collectors out there who appreciate fantastic design, well-executed thinking, and things that make your house look cool. Each volume in this series takes a seminal album and breaks it down in startling minutiae. We love these. We are huge nerds — *Vice*

A brilliant series . . . each one a work of real love — *NME* (UK)

Passionate, obsessive, and smart — *Nylon*

Religious tracts for the rock 'n' roll faithful — *Boldtype*

[A] consistently excellent series — *Uncut* (UK)

We . . . aren't naive enough to think that we're your only source for reading about music (but if we had our way . . . watch out). For those of you who really like to know everything there is to know about an album, you'd do well to check out Bloomsbury's "33 1/3" series of books — *Pitchfork*

For almost 20 years, the 33-and-a-Third series of music books has focused on individual albums by acts well known (Bob Dylan, Nirvana, Abba, Radiohead), cultish (Neutral Milk Hotel, Throbbing Gristle, Wire) and many levels in-between. The range of music and their creators defines 'eclectic', while the writing veers from freewheeling to acutely insightful. In essence, the books are for the music fan who (as Rolling Stone noted) 'thinks liner notes just aren't enough.' — *The Irish Times*

For reviews of individual titles in the series, please visit our blog at 333sound.com and our website at http://www.bloomsbury.com/musicandsoundstudies

Follow us on Twitter: @333books

Like us on Facebook: https://www.facebook.com/33.3books

For a complete list of books in this series, see the back of this book.

Forthcoming in the series:

Shout at the Devil by Micco Caporale
I'm Wide Awake, It's Morning by Holden Seidlitz
Re by Carmelo Esterrich
Tragic Kingdom by Rhae Lynn Barnes
Believe by Lior Phillips
Antics by Gabriel T. Saxton-Ruiz
Carrie & Lowell by Joel Mayward
Weird Al Yankovic in 3-D by Justin Remer
Inflammable Material by Kevin Dunn
I'm Your Baby Tonight by Brandon Tensley
Plastic Beach by Ihor Junyk
Disintegration by Andi Harriman
Dust Bowl Ballads by Allison C. Meier
Blonde by Yousef Srour
Lyburnum Wits End Liberation Fly by Zak Fusciello
So Tonight That I Might See by Anthony Gomez III
What's the 411 by Ricky Tucker

and many more . . .

Cosmic Thing

Pete Crighton

BLOOMSBURY ACADEMIC
NEW YORK • LONDON • OXFORD • NEW DELHI • SYDNEY

BLOOMSBURY ACADEMIC
Bloomsbury Publishing Inc, 1359 Broadway, 12th Floor, New York, NY 10018, USA
Bloomsbury Publishing Plc, 50 Bedford Square, London, WC1B 3DP, UK
Bloomsbury Publishing Ireland, 29 Earlsfort Terrace, Dublin 2, D02 AY28, Ireland

BLOOMSBURY, BLOOMSBURY ACADEMIC and the Diana logo are trademarks of Bloomsbury Publishing Plc

First published in the United States of America 2025
Reprinted 2025

Library of Congress Cataloging-in-Publication Data

Names: Crighton, Pete, author.
Title: Cosmic thing / Pete Crighton.
Description: [1.] | New York : Bloomsbury Academic, 2025. | Series: 33 1/3 | Includes bibliographical references and index. | Summary: "The B-52s fifth record Cosmic Thing took the world by storm in 1989 in the wake of the band's single greatest tragedy: losing guitarist Ricky Wilson to complications from AIDS in 1985. Cosmic Thing is a celebration of queer joy in the face of that seismic setback. Not only did the B-52s have to fight through their pain and grief to make Cosmic Thing, they were up against a conservative government under Reagan (then Bush), a misunderstood virus still ravaging the queer community and the expectations of what 'serious' artists were supposed to look like"--Provided by publisher.
Identifiers: LCCN 2025006385 | ISBN 9798765133125 (paperback) | ISBN 9798765133156 (epub) | ISBN 9798765133149 (pdf)
Subjects: LCSH: B-52's (Musical group). Cosmic thing. | B-52's (Musical group)--History. | New wave music--History and criticism.
Classification: LCC ML421.B052 C75 2025 | DDC 782.42166092/2--dc23/eng/20250212
LC record available at https://lccn.loc.gov/2025006385

ISBN: PB: 979-8-7651-3312-5
ePDF: 979-8-7651-3314-9
eBook: 979-8-7651-3315-6

Series: 33 1/3

Typeset by Deanta Global Publishing Services, Chennai, India
Printed and bound in the Great Britain

For product safety related questions contact productsafety@bloomsbury.com.

To find out more about our authors and books visit www.bloomsbury.com and sign up for our newsletters.

This book is dedicated to
Ricky Wilson, 19 March 1953 – 12 October 1985

Contents

Acknowledgements viii

Introduction 1
1 'Deadbeat Club' 1977–9 11
2 'Dance This Mess Around' 1979–80 29
3 'Deep Sleep' 1981–9 47
4 'Cosmic Thing' 1989–90 77
5 'Keep This Party Going' 1990–2025 105
Conclusion 117

Acknowledgements

Christopher House, you are a gem of a human and partner. Thank you for coping with me on this rollercoaster ride and for your reading and editing help. I love you.

The team at Bloomsbury, in particular Leah Babb-Rosenfeld, thank you for trusting me with this story and for the help and guidance along the way.

Chris Frantz, thank you for making time in your life to talk to me about your experiences with the B-52s. Your insight and candour have made this book so much better.

Ian Gilchrist, I am so grateful to you for connecting me and making my conversation with Chris possible.

Thanks to my friends Andrea Ridgley, Carolyn Taylor, and Ashley and Jeff Wilson who helped me workshop a few ideas included in these pages and make sense of my thoughts.

I am deeply grateful to the quintet of Nicholas Breyfogle, Simon Carpenter, Anne DesBrisay, Jennifer Moroz, and Ken Nyhuus who gave incredible notes on several different drafts to hone this book.

Lisa Whittington-Hill – thank you for talking me off the bridge when I was so very close to the edge.

To the best editor Sarah Piña, I can't wait to see a B-52s show with you!

Introduction

'Cosmic Thing.' 'Planet Claire.' 'There's a Moon in the Sky.' '53 Miles West of Venus.'

The B-52s always had a thing for outer space and interplanetary travel. Which made perfect sense; to me, they were like a blinding flash of light and hope from another planet, aiming directly into my baby gay heart. I was only ten or eleven years old when I first heard 'Rock Lobster' on the radio, and it was like an electric jolt! The B-52s tractor beam caught me and I never wanted to step outside of that glow: I wanted to live on their planet, or in their orbit. These were my people. I have carried the band with me in my heart ever since.

To discover many years later that four of the five band members were queer also made perfect sense: they had always felt like family to me.

'Rock Lobster' is a wild and joyful song and, immediately upon hearing it, I needed to know more about who was making this beautiful noise. Information about your favourite bands wasn't easy to find in the days before the internet – the only real source was your local record store. When I finally held that legendary record cover for the B-52s' eponymous debut in my hands, they looked exactly as they should. With the now famous candy-coated yellow background of the first album cover, their look screamed 'cool' but it also roared 'other'. The B-52s were completely out of step with time. The band was a study in contradictions on that cover: They looked retro, but futuristic. They looked campy, but cool. They looked silly, but sexy.

And within those contradictions, what we all saw, even if it couldn't be named, was queer.

The B-52s were made up of five close friends: Kate Pierson, Fred Schneider, Keith Strickland, and brother-sister combo Cindy and Ricky Wilson. In a 2022 interview with the *LA Times*, Kate acknowledged 'we're a queer band', but for most of the band's career, their queerness was not so overt. It was there but coded; maybe obvious to some, but for a younger me, it took some digging.[1]

The first live gig the fivesome played was at a Valentine's Day party in 1977 – a fitting date, as the B-52s are all heart. What they may have lacked in experience, they made up for by throwing themselves into their art at full force. Wholly committed. Footage of the band playing early gigs and TV appearances is a thing to be seen – they were a wild and untamed beast.

A now infamous *SNL* appearance in early 1980, their first on the show, is a great example of their performance style – throwing themselves around with abandon, Keith pounding on the drums, Ricky playing his custom guitar (duct taped and only four strings!), Kate behind her keyboard, and the three lead singers wailing and flailing with Cindy and Fred hitting the stage floor during 'Rock Lobster'. Heart. It was obvious right from the very beginning.

When I finally got a copy of that first record, purchased at a local strip mall near my parents' home, I devoured every track. From the first note of 'Planet Claire' to the last sounds of clinking glasses and murmuring voices on 'Downtown', I was hooked. I had a new favourite band. Scouring the liner notes only further cemented my love. Amongst the credits for guitar, drums, and so on, I found 'walkie-talkie', 'toy piano', 'smoke alarm', and a credit to 'La Verne for hairdos'. Who were these technicolour crazies? All of a sudden, it seemed to me that anyone could join a band, or perhaps more importantly for me, find the weirdos they needed.

I was only eleven, and I already knew that I didn't quite fit in with the kids at school, that somehow, I was outside the mainstream. I couldn't quite name why I felt that way, but I sure had funny feelings when I stared at Keith on that yellow record cover. I wanted to know him. I wanted to touch him.

While the B-52s quickly found notoriety after that first gig on Valentine's Day, it wouldn't be until twelve years later that they found their greatest commercial success with 1989's *Cosmic Thing*. *Cosmic Thing* was their fifth full-length record and by the time it came out, everyone had pretty much forgotten about the B-52s – including their record label, their management, and most of their fans.

In those intervening years between their first gig and the release of *Cosmic Thing*, the B-52s experienced triumphs and tragedies. The band took the New York scene of the late 1970s by storm, playing at Max's Kansas City and CBGB within months of that first 1977 gig. They released two mid-sized hit albums in 1979 (*The B-52's*) and 1980 (*Wild Planet*) and built a solid reputation as a killer live act; wilder, tougher, and more chaotic than those first two records even suggest.

The Bs seemed a charmed act. But after those first two records, they seemed to lose their footing. A troubled project produced by David Byrne, *Mesopotamia*, ended up as a six-song EP that felt unfinished. Their third and fourth full-length albums, *Whammy!* and *Bouncing Off the Satellites*, have some great highlights but also lacked that ineffable magic that made their first two records so great.

Before *Bouncing Off the Satellites* was released, the band experienced their greatest personal and professional tragedy: Ricky Wilson died, aged thirty-two, on 12 October 1985. Ricky didn't die like 1970s superstars Janis Joplin, Jimi Hendrix, or Jim Morrison – no drugs, no drinking, no overdose. Ricky died of AIDS. His death was a shock to me; it was like losing a friend. The cause wasn't publicly acknowledged in the immediate aftermath of his passing, and the lack of information only added to the confusion of the B-52s' fans. Regardless, the whispers of AIDS came through. Even though Ricky's homosexuality was never overtly acknowledged, there seemed to be no denying it – there was something queer about this band, beyond the beehive wigs and thrift store outfits.

The loss the band must have felt – a band composed not only of close friends but a baby sister as well – is unfathomable. Ricky's talent and his contribution to the B-52s were massive. He was an exceptionally good guitarist, and it was his distinct style of playing, without the two middle strings, that gave the Bs their unique sound in the early days. Many attribute to

Ricky much of the songwriting and arrangements on the band's earliest and best work. How does a band go on after a loss like that? How does anyone pick themselves up after a loved one dies from such a cruel and unpredictable virus? Especially one so misunderstood in 1985? For the B-52s, the answer seemed to be, call it a day.

The band, now reduced to a foursome, made a few reluctant promotional efforts to support *Bouncing Off the Satellites* when it was released in 1986 but refused to tour in support of their new album. With no tour, the record company all but gave up on supporting the record. *Bouncing Off the Satellites* was dead on arrival. It was the lowest charting album of the band's career and it seemed to mark their end.

Their disappearance made the success of *Cosmic Thing* in 1989 and 1990 all the more miraculous. *Cosmic Thing* is a celebration of queer joy against all the odds, against death by a plague still decimating men and women in 1989, against the political conservatism of Reagan and Bush, and against the expectations of what a rock band was supposed to be. Like thousands of queer men and women do every weekend, the Bs wanted to dance their troubles away.

The B-52s had worked with some top-notch producers in their career, including Chris Blackwell and David Byrne, but landing super-producers Nile Rodgers and Don Was to produce *Cosmic Thing* was a stroke of genius, and a pretty big stroke of luck considering where the band was in their career arc. Rodgers in particular was a major coup. He was a monster hit maker, and not just with his own band Chic. Rodgers produced massively popular songs and records for Diana Ross, Madonna, David Bowie, Duran Duran, and

Grace Jones, to name only a few of his superstar credits. Don Was wasn't as well known but he would have his biggest year as a producer in 1989 with *Cosmic Thing* and Bonnie Raitt's massive comeback record *Nick of Time*, the latter winning Album of the Year Grammys for both Was and Raitt.

Two super-producers: check. But did Cindy, Fred, Kate, and Keith have the goods? Boy, did they ever. *Cosmic Thing* was the first record that the band wrote as a unit since their first two albums *The B-52's* and *Wild Planet*. Keith did a lot of advance work and brought a lot of songs in progress to the table. But jamming and bouncing ideas off each other was their secret weapon – a weapon they had lost sight of. They worked best as a team.

Instead of chasing trends, like their previous couple of records (*Whammy!* and *Bouncing Off the Satellites*), the Bs just did their thing: jamming, harmonizing, making great hooks, and working as a unit. It had been nine years since *Wild Planet*, and the Bs were finally living up to the potential hinted at on their second record.

When *Cosmic Thing* was released on 27 June 1989, nobody seemed to really care. It wasn't just their record company that had given up on the B-52s after *Bouncing Off the Satellites*, a lot of fans had too. Out of curiosity and my deep fandom, I dutifully went to the HMV superstore in downtown Toronto and picked up a CD copy on the day of its release. I did not expect much. Imagine my surprise when I heard the most coherent album from the band in almost a decade.

I was twenty years old at that time, still in the closet, and like almost every other B-52s record before it, *Cosmic Thing* was my own private Pride party. I cowered in my closet, terrified of AIDS and the conservatism of the time, assured that sex would kill me and that admitting I was gay would ostracize me. (These were not unreasonable fears as we will explore.)

Like the B-52s' retro/futurism look, *Cosmic Thing* shares a similar duality – the album looks not only backward but also forward. Side one of the record is a nostalgic look at life in Athens before fame and the music industry did its destructive work. Side two concerns itself a bit with the current political climate but mostly looks ahead to a brighter and better world, imagining a queer future.

It's telling that the only Canadian date the B-52s played in support of *Cosmic Thing* on the first leg of their tour was in a shitty club in Mississauga, a suburb outside of Toronto. There wasn't enough interest in them to book a theatre or club downtown. On 16 November 1989, I trekked out to Superstars (the name says it all!) to complete a lifelong goal of seeing the Bs live. The gig was life-changing for me. To see the band was one thing, but to be surrounded by the love and joy the B-52s engendered was my first taste of communal queer love. The Bs rocked that night, and best of all, *Cosmic Thing* ROCKED when played live.

A funny thing happened between buying my ticket to that show and the date of the concert – 'Love Shack' was released as a single on 20 June 1989. Fred admitted he had to go out with the label's A&R team and beg radio stations to play it. They reluctantly did, and soon 'Love Shack' started gaining traction – and fast! The week of that club gig in Mississauga, 'Love Shack' had climbed to #3 on Billboard's Hot 100 chart and became a cultural phenomenon. The song and Cindy's line near its end – *Tin roof . . . rusted!* – took the world by storm. 'Love Shack' and *Tin roof . . . rusted!* were living memes before we even knew what a meme was. A shared cultural experience. And I heard 'Love Shack' everywhere I went.

Another #3 hit song followed with 'Roam' as well as landing the covers of *Rolling Stone* and *SPIN* magazine in March of 1990. Landing a magazine cover, especially *Rolling Stone*, was a big fucking deal. The B-52s would never be the same. The Bs were Big Business all of a sudden.

Cosmic Thing was a smash hit, the likes of which the band had never experienced. That mad success took its toll. By the end of the extensive touring and promoting of the record, Cindy was done. For her, being a B-52 was over, at least for the time being. I can only imagine how brutal it was for her to go on stage, night after night, to sing and play the songs that she and the band had written with her brother, along with the more successful tunes they wrote as a foursome after his death.

The B-52s were down another member. Wilson-less. From five, to four, to three. Not the kind of countdown the fans were hoping for.

The band's legacy following *Cosmic Thing* is a little checkered. They made more missteps than leaps forward, and they sadly seem remembered more for their mistakes.

The B-52s' music, exemplified by *Cosmic Thing*, was the soundtrack to my coming out. Their music and their outrageousness helped me understand the person, and the kind of gay man, I wanted to be. I wanted to be weird. I wanted to make art. I wanted to live outside the mainstream.

I wanted to live on Planet B-52. And it turned out that there were thousands of others like me.

We don't talk enough about the B-52s' queerness. But we should if we want to understand them and what they meant to the world.

As I explore the trials and triumphs of the band through my personal queer lens, I will share my story of coming out and the impact that homophobia, AIDS, and my favourite band had on my development as a queer person. I could talk about what I think queer means for hours, but the two pillars of queerness I want to focus on in these pages are sexual identity and the desire to live outside of mainstream norms and expectations.

Let's queer the B-52s.

A final note before we dive in – to apostrophe, or not apostrophe. When the band started out, they referred to themselves as the B-52's (apostrophe included). Later in their career, they dropped the apostrophe from their name. Throughout this book, I refer to the band as the B-52s (no apostrophe) and continue to identify their first album as *The B-52's* (apostrophe intact). Confused? I was too – another example of this queer little band making it difficult to understand them. Bless their hearts.

Note

1 https://www.latimes.com/entertainment-arts/music/story/2022-11-02/b-52s-retire-tour

1
'Deadbeat Club' 1977–9

Let's go back to the very beginning. The B-52s are one of those bands that are almost impossible to categorize. Punk? Post-punk? New Wave? No Wave? Pop? Rock? Alternative? None of those genres quite capture the B-52s' strange magic. Not even the band's own description as a 'tacky little dance band' does the job. They wore their influences on their sleeve – surf rock, 1960s girl groups, sci-fi film soundtracks, and more – but queered those inspirations to create some of the wildest and most original records to ever grace the Billboard album charts.

While the B-52s felt like they fell out of the sky from another planet, that's not exactly how it happened. The band's origin story is more earth bound but regardless, it contains a certain kind of otherworldliness. Kate Pierson, Fred Schneider, Keith Strickland, Cindy Wilson, and Ricky Wilson – the five members of the B-52s – seemed to work like a utopian collective. The band never had a discernible leader; 40 per cent of the members were women, and the other 60 per cent were gay men. This was not the norm when the band formed in 1977, nor, sadly, is it today.

The B-52s are one of the most unlikely success stories in music history. Proof that sometimes, the good guys win. And sometimes, the good guys are queer.

It all started in the most unlikely places: Athens, Georgia, a small college town in the American South. The B-52s didn't break out of a scene; they created one. Cindy, Keith, and Ricky all grew up in Athens, but Fred and Kate were transplants (both from New Jersey). Keith and Ricky met in high school and became fast friends – best friends in fact – until the day Ricky died. They would play music and record each other in Ricky's teenage bedroom. Ricky and Cindy had also made music and tapes together as kids, so it wasn't long before the kid sister talked her way into playing with the two older boys. The B-52s were never meant to be a trio though. Three lead singers, yes. A trio, no.

Fred and Kate ended up in Athens by fate. (Or by spaceship, who can be sure?) Fred enrolled in the University of Georgia in Athens. Kate ended up on a farm outside of town in a bid to get back to the land and get her hands dirty. She wanted to raise goats and grow her own food and was lucky to find a farm to rent for $15 a month. Irresistible. Maybe Kate was taking Timothy Leary's advice to 'drop out' of the mainstream. Photos of her in those days definitely hint at a hippie-inspired hangover.

Like all weirdos in small towns eventually do, the three Athens natives found Fred and Kate at parties and dances around town. Like magnets, they were drawn to each other. When the band later talked about parties in Athens around that time, it sounded like the little town in Georgia was a southern outpost of Andy Warhol's Factory. Keith describes their friend Jonathan Ayers's parties in *The Guardian* as 'art happenings – walls covered with black plastic; floors thick with popcorn; Beefheart and Velvets records playing. He opened doors to creative possibilities'. Now *that* is the kind of party gone out of bounds I want to get invited to.[1]

Tony Gayton's 1985 film about the music scene in Athens, *Athens GA: Inside/Out*, paints a picture of the small town in his establishing shots. He captures the vibe of small-town, slightly impoverished America – railroad tracks, working and dilapidated farms, kids on skateboards, manual labourers, and a dying main street. While the footage was shot in the mid-1980s, Athens seems lost in time in Gayton's depiction.

Watching the footage now, it seems more representative of the 1960s than life in the 1980s, or at least the 80s I experienced north of the border in Toronto. The film then introduces the audience to a whole cast of artists, the B-52s included, who thrived in the small town, away from the demands of big city living . . . and big city expenses. Gayton's film depicts a time when music and culture were thriving in Athens, in part thanks to the success of the B-52s. In a *Pitchfork* feature by T. Cole Rachel, we are told this about Athens by Fred: 'It was deadly dull, which required that you just make your own fun.'[2]

The five friends clicked and started to get to know each other better while they were crashing parties, getting free drinks, and dancing. It sounds like they were always dancing. Friendship turned into something else one night over a kitschy cocktail at a local Athens restaurant. To hear Kate tell it: 'We shared a big, flaming volcano drink at a Hunan Chinese restaurant, then we jammed that night, and the B-52s were basically born.'[3]

That night, something else extraordinary happened. In the grip of a 'flaming volcano' buzz, the band wrote their first song that night: 'Killer Bees'. Kate later told Frank Gallagher on his podcast *Soundman Confidential*, about how that night became the template for the B-52s' writing process. They would record their uninterrupted jamming and then pick out the best parts from those tapes to create songs.

Five friends became the B-52s that night. Their fate wasn't planned, nobody said 'let's start a band'. Like so many great things in life, it just happened. Kate and Fred have both been quite open about the band's use of pot and mushrooms around this time, and, who knows, maybe those earthbound intoxicants helped loosen the friends' inhibitions.

Keith described the band's democratic approach and their songwriting process in a *SPIN* cover issue from 1990:

> Collective subconscious really comes into play when everyone's improvising . . . 'cause not one person is conceiving of this whole thing. It's coming from five – in the beginning, five different points of view. There's really no leader of the group, because we were a group of friends first, then we started the band. It would have been very odd if all of a sudden someone had said, 'Well, I'm the leader,' or, 'You be the leader.' Friends don't do that. You all work together.[4]

Like so many things in the B-52s' history, the name came from another plane. 'I was having this dream one night', Keith explained to *Rolling Stone*, 'It was about this lounge band that had a woman keyboard player, and she introduced the band as the B-52s. I sprang up out of bed and said, "That's it! The B-52s!" The moniker was fitting since B-52s also happens to be Southern slang for bouffant hairdos'. And bouffant hairdos were very much their thing.[5]

After that first jam, it wasn't long before word spread around the small town about this upstart band. The B-52s booked their first gig in Athens – their friend's Valentine's Day house party on 14 February 1977. Kate described that gig to Frank Gallagher: 'the whole house shook, people were dancing, the house was shaking'.[6] Amazingly, that first house party included early versions of 'Rock Lobster', 'Strobe Light', and 'Planet Claire'. Right from the start, there was clearly something very special happening with this fivesome. Immediately, the B-52s' reputation as a party dancing band was born. Full of heart, creativity, and the joy of working collaboratively.

Their sartorial style was on full display for that first gig, but it wasn't manufactured.

'We always dressed like this', Kate says, trying to explain the campy, kitschy 1960s look that the band's fans so love to imitate. 'We always shopped at thrift stores; it was sort of a pastime. There was a whole group of us in Athens who'd dress this way.'[7]

The band continued to jam, write songs, and have fun together. To challenge each other creatively, they would swap instruments to see what would happen. It didn't matter if anyone had a well-honed skill on any given instrument or not; the challenge and what the shift in energy would inspire were more interesting than finesse. I think that's one of the B-52s' strongest suits: keep people, including themselves, guessing. At its core, though, each of the band members contributed something unique to the recipe: Fred's poems and bent sense of humour, Cindy's raw vocal talent and percussion skills, Ricky and Keith's innate musical sensibility and years of playing together, and Kate's incredible voice and musicianship.

While the band members were still holding down jobs in those early days, nobody was committed to another career. For artists, time and freedom from the demands of a 'career' can yield the most amazing results. The songs the B-52s later wrote about these early days for *Cosmic Thing* are loaded with references to time and freedom to create – crashing parties, drinking cheap beer, playing jukeboxes, skinny dipping, dancing in the rain. Keith had this to say about those times to T. Cole Rachel: 'Our initial inspiration for the band was just to create something for our friends and as a way to entertain ourselves. We had no money and a lot of free time.'[8]

Kevin Hegge's documentary film *Tramps!* elaborates on this idea of time and freedom giving way to creative possibility. *Tramps!* details the scene happening in London during the late 1970s that gave rise to the New Romantics. State-funded art school education, easy access to welfare, and free accommodation from squatting resulted in a bunch of queers and freaks thumbing their noses at the mainstream and creating a vibrant counterculture arts scene.

The late 1970s and early 1980s seem to be the last era that allowed for that kind of activity, especially in the big cities like London, New York, and even Toronto. Urban decay in the 1970s and 1980s saw big population shifts from downtown centres to the suburbs, leaving many empty and hollowed-out buildings for artists to occupy – the last days before commercialism and capitalism took over every aspect of our lives.

The 1970s were an interesting time to be alive. There were still only really four television stations in America and one or two in Canada. Cable TV was a distant dream for most households, mine included. Our generation got snippets of pop culture when we were allowed to watch TV, but for the most part, what was happening in the schoolyard was the only place we got our news and our influences.

I feel sorry for the generation of kids who are tethered to their phones and social media. The proliferation of technology can yield wonderful results, like kids recording entire albums in their bedrooms or making films on their phones, but more often than not, I see the solution to boredom is flipping through Instagram Reels and TikTok and destroying one's self-esteem. I'm not immune; I often find myself reviewing gay Instagram and wishing I were younger, fitter, more handsome, and more successful. Back in the 1970s, though, just like the B-52s, we had to entertain ourselves, and boredom and free time bred creativity. We invented games, we talked and debated, and we roamed the streets unmonitored. We also had to believe whatever was imparted to us by our peers, unchecked by a computer in our pocket. Upsides and downsides.

* * *

During the writing of this book, I had the great pleasure of talking with Chris Frantz, the drummer of Tom Tom Club and Talking Heads. He told me that his wife and bandmate, Tina Weymouth, wanted to highlight that not only were the B-52s incredibly important musically, but they were the first band to bring a drag aesthetic to the mainstream. Weymouth's right. Kate and Cindy's drag-inspired wigs and outfits caused confusion at their early New York shows, with some in the crowd wondering if the two women B-52s members were, in fact, drag queens.

There were many brilliant women fronting bands at the time, like Debbie Harry of Blondie and Pat Benatar. What Cindy and Kate did was different, though. They were part of the band, part of the music, not just front persons. With those wigs, they positioned themselves outside the beauty standards of the day. Unlike many other women in bands, especially the singers, Cindy and Kate were never judged by their beauty or how hot they were – they were just allowed to be themselves. I don't know if it was intentional, but in the process of othering themselves with their wigs and outfits, they queered the press too. Straight men, the entirety of rock and roll press in the 1970s and 1980s, just didn't know what to say about them.

It didn't take long for the B-52s to start making a name for themselves at home and in the much larger city of Atlanta, only about an hour-and-a-half drive from Athens. Chris Frantz told me about meeting the band and his friendship and experiences with the B-52s in the early days. He recalled meeting Cindy, Keith, and Ricky in the late 1970s at a party thrown by the Atlanta band the Fans while on tour with

Talking Heads. Frantz recalled the B-52s that night: 'exuding this sensibility that we (Frantz & Weymouth) felt we had something in common'.[9] Meeting Frantz and Weymouth that night would prove to be a very fortuitous thing for the B-52s.

At Frantz and Weymouth's encouragement, the B-52s headed north to New York City to see if they could find a foothold in the burgeoning punk and post-punk scene happening at CBGB and Max's Kansas City. Atlanta was a whole lot closer to Athens, but the Bs must have known their kind of music would work better amongst the weirdos of NYC.

The band booked their first official gig at Max's Kansas City on 12 December 1977, less than ten months after their first house show on Valentine's Day. Even more amazingly, it would be only their fourth public performance! What's astonishing to me is the confidence that the band had that they could do it. Not that their confidence was ill-founded; the Bs worked hard at their art. They rehearsed four or five days a week and even though they only had a handful of tunes, they honed them, sharpening the rough edges, and turned their improvised jams into tight songs.

Kate told *Interview* magazine in a 1979 feature article that they got paid $17 for their first show at Max's! Gas was cheap in the 1970s, but there is no way they recouped their investment to get up to NYC to play.[10]

Still, the Bs were good enough to get asked back to Max's. And then again. Soon, the B-52s booked the legendary CBGB, and the band began a back and forth between Athens and New York City. Athens is a hell of a commute from New York City – it's a twelve- or thirteen-hour car trip. The five friends were committed though, and started to tamp down a path between the two cities, carting themselves and their gear in Cindy and Ricky's parents' station wagon. That's devotion, that's heart. Of those early shows, Chris Frantz said 'They were still pretty rough around the edges . . . you could just tell this was something very promising.'[11] The B-52s were on their way.

Culturally, those first few years of the B-52s' existence were strange times. There seemed to be hints of queerness bubbling up into the mainstream, but even this author, who turned ten in 1979, sensed that anything remotely gay was the butt of the joke, not to be taken seriously. Television shows like *Hollywood Squares* regularly featured closeted gay men making coded gay jokes about themselves.

The music scene was turning on a dime. The year 1977 saw the release of one of the most popular records of all time – Fleetwood Mac's *Rumours*. A cultural phenomenon, it was ubiquitous in 1977, and maybe Fleetwood Mac made the world safe for bands with three lead singers? Three lead singers, two female and one male, was about the only thing Fleetwood Mac and the B-52s would ever have in common.

The year also featured piles of records from the old guard ruling the airwaves and the charts. Bands like the Eagles, Steve Miller Band, Foreigner, Pink Floyd, and one of the weirdest rock and roll albums to ever hit number one, Meatloaf's *Bat Out of Hell* (a rock opera steeped in camp, I loved it!) had a stranglehold on the charts.

The old guard may have ruled the airwaves and sales charts, but 1977 also saw the release of records by bands who were moving the culture dial significantly. The Sex

Pistols, The Clash, Talking Heads, and the Ramones all released new albums – debuts by all but the last. Fleetwood Mac may have made the world safe for bands with three lead singers, but these punk and cutting-edge bands were making the world safe for the B-52s musically. I turned eight in 1977, and I was already starting to pay attention to the avant-garde. My record collection wouldn't include the Sex Pistols or the Clash for a few more years, but *Talking Heads 77* found its way into my collection soon after I bought *The B-52s*. I played 'Psycho Killer' and 'Pulled Up' non-stop, and still do.

By 1978, disco had not only gone mainstream but had taken over as the dominant force in popular music, thanks mostly to the enormous success of the *Saturday Night Fever* soundtrack featuring several era-defining hits by the Bee Gees. Before it hit the mainstream, though, disco was the sound of gay clubs. The genre was originated by Black and Latinx artists and catered to outsiders, but, of course, it took three cute white boys to move disco into the mainstream.

Sylvester, a disco artist who challenged the gender binary in ways the world wasn't ready for, released his debut record in 1977 and his legendary *Step II* album in 1978. I wouldn't hear about Sylvester or his queerness for many years, and his records did not rocket to the top of the charts like the Bee Gees. The Village People, however, were a wildly popular disco act during the late 1970s. They were a manufactured band featuring five stereotypes of gay men, packaged up for straight folks. The Village People were far more successful than Sylvester but had their queerness erased. They were a cartoon band for straight people, singing about gay themes like going to the 'Y.M.C.A.' and being a 'Macho Man'. Very confusing for us young closeted boys.

During the disco craze, a young Nile Rodgers, future producer of *Cosmic Thing*, and his band Chic had their first number one song with 'Freak Out' in 1978. (9 December 1978).

Outside of the mainstream, though, queers were starting to make art that truly reflected our experiences. Derek Jarman and John Waters were making films in the United Kingdom and United States respectively that were queer as fuck but not easy to find. Watching Jarman's *Jubilee* (1978) or any of Waters' films now is like watching a queer revolution in real time. But those films were not getting mainstream attention or hitting the schoolyard grapevine. It would be years before I discovered either of these queer artists.

In 1977 and 1978 I wasn't flinging myself around up on stage like the B-52s, but like the good little homosexual I was, I could be found throwing myself around a gymnastics gym . . . and listening to the Bee Gees! I was excellent at gymnastics; I was fearless, wildly flexible, and full of determination. But doing that sport was akin to wearing a target on my back that said *Faggot – Kick Me*. I didn't even know what a faggot was but the kids at school sure seemed to, and they had no problem telling me that I was one. My budding gymnastics career did not last long, the first of a few things I would put aside for fear of being bullied and targeted as gay. I put my head in the sand and bought records instead.

I wasn't the only one in 1977 suffering from bullying and homophobia – the B-52s were being targeted in their hometown too. Kate recounted in a 2020 interview with *Juice Magazine*: 'When we first played in Athens, we were walking down to this bar and there were college students and jocks and they threw a brick at us and said, "Queers!"'[12]

The long fight for gay rights was well underway by this time, but the only thing I heard about gay people in the late 1970s was about them getting bullied, beaten, and arrested. Toronto had a rather infamous gay bar called The St. Charles Tavern on Yonge Street, a main thoroughfare through downtown. Stories of high school kids heading down to Yonge Street to pelt the 'faggots' with eggs as they entered or exited the bar were passed around the schoolyard daily. I was internalizing that it was normal for gay men to be bullied.

I wouldn't hear about Anita Bryant for several years, but it was in 1977 that she got slapped in the face with a cream pie by gay rights protestors for her homophobic rants. She deserved that pie-in-the-face, and it is thankfully captured on film for all of us to enjoy again and again. But gay men and women fighting back was not the kind of news being shared in my schoolyard. I wouldn't even hear about the Stonewall riots for decades.

Me and my classmates should have been laughing at Anita getting pied, but instead we were laughing at one of the most homophobic television shows ever aired. *Three's Company* premiered in March of 1977 and is as vile as any of Anita Bryant's anti-gay rants. John Ritter starred as a straight man pretending to be gay so that he could live with two single young women. That three adults had to fool their landlord to live together is an indicator of how prudish the times still were. That was the central joke of the show – John Ritter prancing and mincing around like a caricature of what people thought gay men were, for laughs. Suffice it to say, it has not aged well, and its offences deserve their own book. We all thought it was hilarious.

They were truly strange times, and they provided the perfect backdrop for the B-52s' rise to fame. There was a subset of weirdos out there that was ready for something fresh and new.

With each and every gig, the B-52s were solidifying their reputation as a killer live act, and with good reason. Thanks to the wonders of YouTube, there is footage of a set the B-52s played at the Downtown Cafe in Atlanta on 2 September 1978 – only eighteen months after that first Valentine's Day gig. It's incredible to see how fully formed the band is. The footage includes seven songs: '52 Girls', 'Hero Worship', 'Devil in My Car', 'Downtown', 'Dance This Mess Around', 'Running Around', and 'Rock Lobster'.[13]

The footage is fantastic considering it's over forty years old. The camera work focuses on the three singers, with Keith visible behind them, pounding away on his drum kit. Ricky is mostly lost on stage right. The interplay of the three vocalists is so great; the way they give each other focus, moving to the side of the stage to let another vocalist have the attention of the crowd. It looks miraculously ego-less and to me, that's queer – letting the spotlight shine on your friends and lifting each other up rather than trying to take the focus for yourself.

Fred looks like a waif of a thing, in need of a few good meals – a skinny young man in a singlet flailing around on stage like a man possessed. It's hard to watch this now and think Fred is anything *but* gay, however those were the times: gays were hiding in plain sight. Kate's wearing the shirt she has on the *Wild Planet* cover, and Cindy is mostly hiding underneath her mess of a wig. I suspect Cindy liked it that way. Ricky and Keith are locked into position playing guitar and drums, respectively, but it's awesome to see the other three in motion. Cindy bashing away at her tambourine and Fred behind the keyboard for 'Hero Worship' and '52 Girls' allowing Kate to play guitar on those two tracks. Teamwork at its best.

The songs all sound well practised, as though they'd been playing them for years. For a band often pigeonholed as a new wave act, it's pure rock and roll abandon up on that stage in Atlanta. They are wild, dancing, and out of control in the best way. The crowd is eating it up and going crazy! Bouncing up and down non-stop, they are clearly loving what they are hearing and seeing.

The only thing the band was really lacking at this point in their career was some decent stage banter! This lack of imagination can be heard on the *B-52s Live! 8-24-79* album. Fred's the only one to really address the audience, and his go-to comment is 'this is another dance song'. It would take some time for this group of introverted extroverts to get over their shyness. Cindy and Kate's vocals sound a bit rough around the edges, but it's the entire band's commitment that sells it. Hot damn, they were sizzling hot and full of heart.

With the band gaining fans and momentum, the B-52s decided it was time to release a single. They chose 'Rock Lobster' and '52 Girls' to record and worked with their friend Danny Beard, who created DB Records, to release it. The Bs managed to sell 20,000 copies of that single at gigs and independent record stores, and Beard went on to release singles by many other Athens- and Atlanta-based artists.

Those early versions are available on YouTube and the sound is a little more primitive, heavier on the cowbell, but for all intents and purposes, 'Rock Lobster' sounds like it did on their debut album. It has the same harmonies, the same guitar part, and the same Yoko Ono-inspired wailing by Cindy and Kate. '52 Girls' was also a bit more raw sounding than the album version, but it was ready for the big leagues too.

This was a band ready for the recording studio. And ready for a much bigger stage.

Notes

1 https://www.theguardian.com/music/article/2024/jul/22/limbo-district-band-athens-michael-stipe-rem-b52s-dominique-amet-davey-stevenson-kelly-crow

2 https://www.tcolerachel.com/b-52s

3 https://www.newyorker.com/magazine/2023/10/16/the-b-52s-back-on-the-boardwalk, published in the print edition of the 16 October 2023, issue, with the headline 'Pinball Wizard'.

4 SPIN Magazine Vol. 5, No. 12, March 1990.

5 https://www.rollingstone.com/music/music-features/interview-the-b-52s-113100/2/

6 https://podcastaddict.com/soundman-confidential/episode/117014064

7 https://www.rollingstone.com/music/music-features/interview-the-b-52s-113100/4/

8 https://www.tcolerachel.com/b-52s

9 Chris Frantz interview, Aug 22, 2024.

10 https://www.interviewmagazine.com/music/the-b-52s-beehives-not-bombers

11 Chris Frantz interview, Aug 22, 2024.

12 https://juicemagazine.com/home/the-b-52s-kate-pierson-talks-sci-fi-surf-culture-groovy-music-lazy-desert-and-thrift-store-chic/

13 https://www.youtube.com/watch?v=B-TEhBWdtKA

2
'Dance This Mess Around' 1979–80

With the increasing buzz from live gigs and the success of DB Records' release of 'Rock Lobster', major record labels started to express interest in signing this wild new dance band.

Kate told *Rock Cellar Magazine* that 'People came down from Virgin Records. Seymour Stein came down to Athens to see us and he kind of wooed us. Our thought was, "Wow, free dinner!"' Everybody loves a free meal but it wasn't Virgin or Stein's Sire Records that landed the B-52s.[1]

With the sharks circling, Chris Frantz and Tina Weymouth had a hand in helping the B-52s get a record deal and a manager too. When Frantz and Weymouth were in Nassau making the second Talking Heads album, *More Songs About Buildings and Food*, in 1978, Chris Blackwell, head of Island Records, asked them for some advice. Frantz recalled Blackwell asking him and his wife 'if you were to sign any band in America now, who would that be?'[2] Frantz responded with his brother's band, Urban Verbs and the B-52s.

Frantz and Weymouth's efforts didn't stop there. The pair introduced the Bs to Talking Heads manager Gary

Kurfirst, who had a long and fruitful history with Blackwell and Island Records. Before long, the B-52s were signed to a management deal with Kurfirst and inked a North American record deal with Warner Bros. Records, leaving Blackwell's Island Records handling the international territories. The B-52s were on their way!

Blackwell wasn't just interested in the B-52s for his label; he wanted to produce the band's debut record too. As head of Island, he could have chosen any of the bands in his roster to produce, but something about the B-52s must have piqued his curiosity. Like Chris Frantz, Blackwell clearly saw something special in this upstart new band.

With more than enough songs at the ready, honed from constant gigging, it was time to get this band in the studio. Very quickly, the B-52s found themselves at Compass Point Studios in Nassau, Bahamas to record their first album. Nassau must have felt like a very long way away from downtown Athens, or Kate's farm without running water. Can you imagine the B-52s on the beach, lazing under a palm tree, or swimming in the Caribbean? What happens to those wigs when they get wet?

Kate told Frank Gallagher that Blackwell wanted to 'let them sound exactly like they sound' when he recorded them.[3] The band's infectious energy jumps out at you, the tunes were timeless, and Blackwell was wise to stand out of the way and capture the band in its purest form.

Almost the entire album was recorded live in the studio, with the band playing whatever instruments they did during their stage shows. That meant Kate playing guitar parts on '52 Girls' and 'Hero Worship', Cindy playing guitar on

'There's a Moon in the Sky (Called the Moon)' and Fred doing the keyboard bass part on 'Hero Worship'. Other band members had more technical prowess on those instruments, but Blackwell was more interested in capturing the B-52s' vibe, more so than the perfect take. I love that Blackwell wanted to recreate the band's live sound so devotedly. That approach harkened back to those early jams when they would pass instruments around to challenge each other and spark creativity.

There were a few overdubs, but, for the most part, what we hear on that debut record is what the band recorded to tape, live in the studio. It's an incredible feat for a band who wasn't necessarily known for their technical prowess, but once again, their heart, dedication, and enthusiasm won out.

I'm sure the masters for the eponymously named album were delivered, and the record company wondered 'what the fuck are we going to do with this?' Disco was still the hot commercial trend of the day in 1979, and no doubt the publicity team was stumped. The B-52s were *not* Disco.

The best way to start promoting the album was to release the song that sold out its independent run of singles and drove crowds mental: 'Rock Lobster'. It turned out to be an astute, if blindingly obvious, choice. 'Rock Lobster' became a sensation! Nowhere more so than in my native Canada. There was something about 'Rock Lobster' us Canadians couldn't resist. The song only made it as high as #56 on Billboard's Hot 100 chart in the United States but 'Rock Lobster' rocketed to number one on Canada's national singles chart RPM in May of 1980.[4]

The first time I heard 'Rock Lobster' on the radio, in a car with an older friend, Deanne, it was a strange awakening. The song was wild, it was nonsensical, but I knew that it was mine, that the band made the song for me, and others like me. Hearing 'Rock Lobster' was like being struck by a lightning bolt! Immediately, I needed to hear more music from the B-52s.

I broke open my piggy bank, an old-timey stagecoach affair, and counted up my quarters and dimes. I had enough money saved to buy my first record with my very own money. My musical awakening had just begun with 'Rock Lobster'.

Before I could even get the record home, I stared at that iconic yellow cover. Who the hell were these people? The background – an almost fluorescent yellow glow – with the retro *High Fidelity* logo in the top left corner and the outrageous-looking outfits, all spelled out that something new had arrived. The B-52s not only sounded like nothing else on earth, they looked it too.

The cover photo by George DuBose came from a February 1979 issue of *Interview* magazine. DuBose took the photo in his studio simply because he liked the band and wanted to help them out – and he perfectly captured the sense of cool and campiness of the B-52s. DuBose printed a thousand copies of the photo, designed with enough white space for the band to write gig details on, but anytime they were put up around New York, they'd get stolen immediately. When it came time to choose a cover image for their first album, the Bs smartly wanted to use the same photo, and this time George got paid $750! A steal. The original photo was black and white, so Island decided to colourize it – resulting in one of the most iconic album covers of all time. Island got a deal on that photo. Poor George didn't even get a photo credit on the album.[5]

The article that accompanied that iconic photo in *Interview* magazine is a great example of how the press were talking about the B-52s at the time. It references the band's wigs, UFOs, being on the road, and all sorts of goofing around; in fact, the interviewer seems more interested in the B-52s aesthetic and influences than he is in the music. Something that the band would constantly struggle with for the rest of their career.[6]

Once I peeled the shrink wrap off the cover of my album, the inside sleeve carried some more hints that this band was out of the ordinary. The eye-popping canary yellow background carries over to the inside sleeve with red text detailing the lyrics, the band members, and the instruments played on the album. The photos of the instruments were a bit of a mind-fuck, though: Why is there a walkie-talkie with Morse code instructions on it and a duct-taped old guitar with a few missing strings? We'd soon find out that the technicolour explosion extended to their sound too.

I pulled the black vinyl disc out of the yellow sleeve to see the instruction PLAY LOUD printed on both sides of the matching yellow album label. Alright then. It turned out to be great advice. Oftentimes, records need time to carve their way into my heart, but I was sold immediately on the B-52s. Every note. Every word. I was hooked.

Beyond that fluorescent yellow cover, how is *The B-52's* queer? Let's take a closer look at their queerness in both sexual identity and outsider status, and their incredible musicianship.

'Planet Claire' – The first sound I heard on the record when I dropped the needle on side one is a distant beeping. Is it Morse code from the walkie-talkie pictured on the inner sleeve? Is it a message from outer space? Likely the latter. With that first 'beep, beep, beep', the B-52s unknowingly charted their interstellar course. 'Planet Claire' is a blazing track and the perfect way to introduce audiences to their off-beat musical sensibilities. The song takes its time, building the space-age mood; Kate's voice has an effect on it as she harmonizes with the organ, and it's not until after the two-and-a-half-minute mark that we hear any recognizable voice or word from Fred: *She came from Planet Claire.* What an introduction! A loud and proud declaration that the B-52s were different.

'52 Girls' – Girls, singing about girls! In 1979, women in a band with men, singing about other women, was revolutionary. Even if '52 Girls' is primarily a list of names, the B-52s passed the Bechdel test before it was even invented! When I listen to it today, I love to imagine it as a list of an alpha lesbian's weekend conquests.

'Rock Lobster' – I didn't know it when I first heard it, but those wails, barks, grunts, and shrieks near the end of the song by Cindy and Kate are pure Yoko Ono. Neither I nor the mainstream had any idea of their inspiration, but Yoko fandom is queer, it just is. Fight me. Boys in bikinis! What world was this the Bs were living in? I wanted in.

'Lava' – The B-52s' first horny track! Despite Fred's insistence on *Live! 8.24.1979* that this is a song about a volcano, it's pretty obvious that this is a paean to male orgasm. The girls aren't left out of the fun, though – they too have a need for release. It's likely not the first time semen was likened to *red hot lava*, but never before or since has it been done so effectively. Hearing a man sing about watching another man (we assume) blow a load was revolutionary.

'There's a Moon in the Sky (Called the Moon)' – A message of hope I didn't even know I needed was on track two on the second side of the album: *'cause there are thousands of others like you.* A coded rallying cry for other queers. Even though I felt very alone in my bedroom or amongst the peers in my class, I trusted Fred. I wasn't entirely sure what he meant, but I knew deep down that I wanted to find the others like me. I intuitively knew that when I found them, they were also going to be B-52s fans.

'6060-842' – There is something so transgressive about making Tina the horny caller in this song. A woman with sexual needs calling a number scribbled on a bathroom wall? Out of sync with the times, even today, it's a perfect twist on a fun and rocking Bs classic.

'Hero Worship' – The first Bs song with lyrics by their friend Robert Waldrop, this track is pure, unbridled punk energy. Cindy's commitment and heart result in an indelible vocal performance. There isn't a single track like 'Hero Worship' on the band's first album, and we wouldn't hear it again, quite frankly. It's a revelation.

Only a week after *The B-52's* was released came the infamous 'Disco Demolition Night' in Chicago. The anti-disco movement had been gaining some traction in the public consciousness, and it reached its tipping point on 12 July 1979, thanks to Chicago radio DJ Steve Dahl. He was so contemptuous of disco that Dahl used a pronounced lisp when he spoke the word on air, showing clear disdain of the genre, and of homosexuals. The Chicago White Sox partnered with Dahl on a promotion where fans could get a discounted ticket to a double-header game if they brought a disco record with them. Dahl would then detonate the pile of records in between the two games. The event took place in Chicago's White Sox stadium on the south side of the city, a predominantly Black neighbourhood, rather than Wrigley Field on the north side of the city.[7]

During the demolition display, a bunch of angry, mostly white, male rock fans took the opportunity to riot for the most ridiculous reason in rioting history – imagine rioting against disco? The subtext wasn't too hard to read – disco was a genre built by Black and Latinx communities and enjoyed by gay men before exploding into the mainstream with all manner of people enjoying the genre at clubs like Studio 54. The beauty of disco was its ability to bring so many disparate communities together, joyfully mingling and doing 'The Hustle' side by side. The 'Disco Demolition Night' has long been considered a homophobic and racist act both for the genre targeted and the choice of neighbourhood where it took place. Future *Cosmic Thing* producer, Nile Rodgers, went so far as to liken the event to a Nazi book burning. Watching Major League Baseball host gay Pride nights today just makes me laugh. (But it's a start, I suppose.)[8]

It's a good thing *The B-52's* was a guitar-driven dance record, or the Bs' career might have been over before it even started. Disco still had some life in it though. Nile Rodgers and his band Chic would have their second (of two) number one hits with the legendary 'Good Times', from Chic's third album in August of 1979. Disco may not have been dead, but the warning shots were fired by the 'Disco Demolition Night'. My schoolyard would soon be full of *Disco Sucks* T-shirts.

With their debut album on record store shelves, the B-52s went out on their first proper tour of America and Europe, paired with Talking Heads. That friendship with Frantz and Weymouth, and a shared manager, proved its worth again. Can you imagine seeing that pairing? Talking Heads touring their newly released third record *Fear of Music* and the B-52s promoting their first. What a double bill!

The buzz kept building for the B-52s thanks to constant touring, but it was their appearance on *Saturday Night Live* (*SNL*) on 26 January 1980 that proved to be the game changer. In the years before MTV, there weren't that many opportunities for any band on American TV at the time, and landing *SNL* was a real coup. Good job, Gary Kurfirst.

The band played two songs that night on *SNL* – 'Dance This Mess Around' and 'Rock Lobster'. 'Dance This Mess Around' was never a single release but it was a fan favourite. Cindy's vocals are a bit rough-edged, but she is positively going for it and sells the performance with her usual heart and commitment. Kate's vocals are a bit more accomplished by this point, and she sounds a little more solid than Cindy.

'Rock Lobster' is perfection. Fred is banging away on the cowbell and the whole band is alive with energy. The song is bonkers enough, but when Fred and Cindy drop to the ground during the 'down, down' section, the viewing audience must have been thinking *what the fuck is this*? A legendary dance craze was born that night – every time I hear 'Rock Lobster' at a party, someone (oftentimes me, quite honestly) hits the floor when the song instructs us 'down, down'.

For a band remembered for their wild looks, the Bs' outfits were not that outrageous on *SNL* that night. Cindy's wearing 1950s-inspired pants and a sleeveless shirt with a big blonde wig (or two, maybe three wigs), and Kate's wearing a green dress and red cone wig. It's the three gay men who are dressed most conservatively. Fred's pencil-thin moustache and seersucker suit jacket matched with a pale blue T-shirt and slacks looks a bit anachronistic, but the overall effect is pretty tame. Ricky's indigo outfit and Keith's green shirt and black pants combo look . . . dare I say it, *normal*. Kate and Cindy's wigs are the strangest-looking things on stage. I can't help but wonder if the men were hiding a bit with their muted dress: the mainstream likely wasn't ready for three guys in wigs.

To hear Kate tell it, the band was terrified but undaunted, and their now iconic performance pushed them into a new level of fame and success. *The B-52's* climbed the charts following *SNL* and word started to spread. This little underground band was starting to make some mainstream noise.

The B-52s likely could have ridden the success of 'Rock Lobster' and their first album a little longer. I suspect the success caught the band and the record company by surprise; the increased exposure from the *SNL* appearance and the constant touring paid off big time. Suddenly, the B-52s had a gold record. Something that even their friends and touring partners Talking Heads hadn't achieved yet!

By the time 'Rock Lobster' hit number one in Canada that May of 1980, the band already had another album in the can!

Only thirteen months after the release of that first record, the B-52s followed up with *Wild Planet* in August of 1980.

Wild Planet meant another trip to Nassau, and I suppose, another suitcase full of soggy wigs. Chris Blackwell oversaw the proceedings as executive producer but brought in Rhett Davies to work with the band too. The B-52s were keeping very good company. Davies was an innovative British producer who had worked with a host of bands who were pushing the sound envelope, including Roxy Music, Talking Heads, and Brian Eno. Davies brought a little bit more polish to the Bs sound. The first record captured them as they sounded live, *Wild Planet* sounds more like a studio effort.

Thanks to the amazing songs and the incredible work of the band with Blackwell and Davies, there would be no sophomore slump for the B-52s. *Wild Planet* is an accomplished work and still sounds remarkably contemporary today.

The first thing I noticed about the *Wild Planet* album cover was the vibrant red colour! It would be forever known as *the red album* amongst my friends (similarly, the first was *the yellow album*). Another 1960s-inspired icon is placed in the top right corner – a dodecagram, a twelve-pointed shape that's often used to symbolize creativity, balance, and harmony; the Bs were getting deeper. The blue B-52s logo vibrates in contrast to the red! The *Wild Planet* cover is gorgeous, and it looks like the B-52s are at the coolest cocktail party ever.

The photograph on the cover is the most straightforward image of the band to appear on their album jackets. Kate's cone-shaped wig is the only real sign of camp or craziness; even Cindy's wig is a pretty mellow black number. Kate's outfit is retro but nothing too wild, and the rest of the band is dressed mostly in black, looking sharp. The boys all look handsome – in particular my boy Keith holding a transistor radio (or maybe the walkie-talkie from the first album sleeve?). Was this a band looking to be taken seriously? The only downside for me personally is that Fred looked a whole lot like a teacher in my school who would later turn into a personal tormentor – more on that later.

The inside sleeve is a deep green colour covered with paw prints and scratches from animal claws, an obvious sign that *Wild Planet* is just that: untamed. The music is feeding our base instincts, our animalistic urges, and our desires.

Just like the first record, before I can drop the needle on the turntable, they've given their listening instructions in bold letters on the record label – PLAY LOUD. Advice I recommend that people heed every time they listen to the B-52s. *Wild Planet* sounds GREAT, especially when it's PLAYED LOUD!

Unlike the slow build from a distant planet of the first album, *Wild Planet* starts with a bang: the unmistakable nasal drone of Fred declaring *SURPRISE*! on album opener 'Party Out of Bounds', followed by the next word we hear – *PARTY*. It is unmistakably party time, and the Bs never look back from that starting point. The energy is unrelenting. While *The B-52's* had a few horny moments on it, 'Lava' being the most obvious, *Wild Planet* ups the ante tenfold!

Let's look at my favourite queer moments and coded messages built into *Wild Planet*!

'Dirty Back Road' – Robert Waldrop pops up again as the lyricist on 'Dirty Back Road' and is credited with art direction on the back cover. While not an official member of the band, Waldrop's name sure pops up a lot. 'Dirty Back Road' is a sexy slow-jam compared to the opener but it still sizzles. It's dangerous. It's sexy. It's southern. And it's almost undoubtedly about getting fucked. In the butt. It's not too hard to use one's imagination to think about what the dirty back road is exactly. Though Kate and Cindy sing the following line, let's not forget it's a man who wrote it: *Like a road, You ride me.*

It's a wild and reckless track and we're told *Don't look back.* Why? What are we running from?

'Private Idaho' – This whole track is a perfect metaphor for living in the closet. Apologies to the Idahoans who might be reading this, but being stuck in Idaho is a pretty apt metaphor for being trapped somewhere you don't want to be. When Fred asks *Where do I go from here, to a better state than this?*, it's like a window into my mind in 1980; how *do* I get to a better state? The way Cindy uses her voice – modulating the syllables of *Idaho* feels very much like the torture of being trapped in the closet. Confused. In a whirlpool.

Where exactly is this pool full of strangers that's fraught with danger that Fred's singing about? Can someone send me an address, please?

'Devil in My Car' – The devil in 'Devil in My Car' is very likely a substitute for being queer. We're on a *freeway to Hell* and *don't want to go to Hell.* When Fred screams *I don't want to go to the Devil,* I think we can all figure out what he means without too much trouble. It's often how we feel when we're fighting our desire, or, in fact, how I felt for a few decades on the other side of that closet door. I would have traded identities with any of my straight peers in a heartbeat but, unlike Fred, I kept my screams inside my own head. My personal confrontation with the devil was at least a decade away.

'Quiche Lorraine' – Truly, could a heterosexual write a song about a 2-inch-tall poodle in designer jeans named Quiche Lorraine *and* sing it with such dedication, absent of all camp, and in the process make it the most camp thing possible? I wonder which of Fred's ex-boyfriends inspired 'Quiche Lorraine?' He must have been one bad dog.

'Strobe Light' – Maybe one of the most overt sex songs in the B-52s' whole catalogue. While the dialogue is mostly between Fred and the harmonies of Kate and Cindy, I love how dispassionate the two women are at the thought of sex with a man! Fred's instructions to lay on the floor and make love under a strobe light, however, predates some of the very specific Grindr messages I would receive thirty years later. Trust me, I have received far stranger requests than having sex under a flashing strobe light.

And Fred wants to kiss the *Pineapple*? We all understand he was talking about female breasts, but the pineapple is also the universal symbol for swingers. Maybe the Bs were telling us *anything goes* in their sphere.

'Give Me Back My Man' – Though this track isn't necessarily all that queer, it deserves mention as one of the greatest songs in the B-52s catalogue. *I'll give you fish, I'll give you candy, I'll give you everything I have in my hand.* Cindy sings the hell out of this song, taking the nonsensical lyrics and turning them into real human emotion, desperation mostly. A plea to a lost lover, 'Give Me Back My Man' aches, and after Ricky's death, I now can't help but hear a plea to bring back the dead. 'Give Me Back My Man' is epic.

Wild Planet built on the momentum started by the first album and shot into the top twenty of Billboard's album charts. The Bs second album would reach #18 on 18 October 1980 besting the band's first record's top position of #59. A huge improvement.[9]

Several weeks after *Wild Planet* hit its peak chart position, John Lennon and Yoko Ono released a new album, partly inspired by 'Rock Lobster', that would soon shoot to number one. *Double Fantasy* was released on 17 November 1980, and Lennon declared the B-52s to be his favourite band, citing 'Rock Lobster' as the inspiration for getting back into the studio with Ono. No small praise.[10]

Lennon didn't live long enough to enjoy the success of *Double Fantasy*; he was murdered on 8 December 1980, only weeks after the album's release. I was only eleven but can still remember hearing the shocking news on the baseball diamond of my elementary school and thinking *it can't be true*. It was the first time a celebrity's death hit home for me. Most of us 1970s kids grew up with The Beatles, and his death rattled us and the world at large. It was a sure sign that the party decade of the 1970s was over.

Margaret Thatcher had been elected prime minister of the UK in 1979, the year *The B-52's* was released, and Ronald Reagan was nominated as president of the United States of America in 1980, the year *Wild Planet* was released. Both elections spelled troubling times ahead for queer people or anyone living outside the mainstream. There was a storm on the horizon. Staunch conservatism was on the rise, and the yuppie decade was about to start. Thatcher and Reagan's elections gave new life to capitalism, privatization, and religion. Thanks but no thanks 1979.

Disco was breathing its last breath with Diana Ross's 'I'm Coming Out.' Produced by Nile Rodgers (naturally) and his partner Bernard Edwards, the song wasn't meant to be a gay anthem, but boy, did it become one. In Canada, we were puzzling over 'High School Confidential' by Rough Trade and their iconic singer Carole Pope. A woman singing about creaming her jeans over another female classmate. I was busy trying to hide myself. Diana Ross and Rough Trade were way too gay for me.

The bestselling record of 1980 was Pink Floyd's *The Wall*. A double album about alienation and losing a grip on reality was a sure sign that things were getting serious in the 1980s. Trying to fit in with the straight boys at school, I bought *The Wall* and Bruce Springsteen's *The River* (also released that year) and ignored Diana Ross and Carole Pope. Which of the four do you think I listen to more now?

The B-52s were blazing hot, and at eleven, I was a huge fan. Where would we all fit into the decade ahead?

Notes

1 https://rockcellarmagazine.com/kate-pierson-the-b52s-interview-rock-lobster/

2 Chris Frantz interview, Aug 22, 2024.

3 https://podcastaddict.com/soundman-confidential/episode/117014064

4 https://www.bac-lac.gc.ca/eng/discover/films-videos-sound-recordings/rpm/Pages/image.aspx?Image=nlc008388.0169a&URLjpg=http%3a%2f%2fwww.collectionscanada.gc.ca%2fobj%2f028020%2ff4%2fnlc008388.0169a.gif&Ecopy=nlc008388.0169a

5 https://george-dubose.com/en/category/the-b52s

6 https://www.interviewmagazine.com/music/the-b-52s-beehives-not-bombers

7 https://www.chicagotribune.com/2020/12/18/commentary-disco-and-the-bee-gees-are-beloved-today-but-as-disco-demolition-night-and-a-new-hbo-documentary-demonstrate-that-wasnt-true-40-years-ago/

8 https://www.independent.co.uk/news/world/americas/disco-inferno-680390.html

9 https://www.billboard.com/artist/the-b-52s-2/

10 https://www.dailymail.co.uk/tvshowbiz/article-7242807/The-B-52s-guitarist-Keith-Strickland-reveals-tragic-death-nearly-ended-group.html

3
'Deep Sleep' 1981–9

After the initial rush of two incendiary albums in as many years, the bulk of the 1980s was a frustrating time to be a B-52s fan. It felt like we were being fed tidbits, snack-sized portions of new B-52s material, and nothing was quite as satisfying as their first two records. There was plenty of gold to be mined from the band's output during 1981–6 but each release sounded rushed or incomplete. I wanted a full album that lived up to the promise of the one-two punch of *The B-52's* and *Wild Planet*. For that, I would have to wait a while.

Before I start this chapter, I feel I have to profess my deep love for all of the projects contained herein. Deep and unwavering love. However, they are all far from the B-52s' best work. As much as it pains me to critique their efforts, I feel I must.

*** *Party Mix!* 1981 ***

To help keep fans engaged with the B-52s after the *Wild Planet* album, the first stop-gap measure was 1981's *Party*

Mix!, released in July. A six-song EP of remixed and reworked tracks from the first two records, *Party Mix!* was a blast.

Not only was the record fun, but it also featured another indelible album cover from the band. First, we saw yellow, next came red. For *Party Mix!* we got green – the first move away from primary colours! I was into it! Each of the band members is posed in what looks like a combination of early green screen work meets kindergarten cut and paste. Kate's waving to (or maybe saluting?) some alien overlords in a beauty of a beehive wig and sporting a fitted green dress over a black body stocking. Ricky is leaning over a bench looking a bit forlorn, I get the sense his joy was in making music and not the publicity side of the business. Fred is wearing an oversized red satin-looking jacket paired with tuxedo pants featuring red piping and, quite frankly, looks surprised, if not downright annoyed, that we've invaded his little party. As usual, Keith looks the most muted in his white shirt, black pants, and New Balance sneakers. There is some random clothing, a handbag, and a lava lamp littered around the band, and it almost looks like we busted in on a B-52s dress-up party – or their change room at the local thrift store. The kind of party, or scene, that I was desperately hoping to be invited to.

Cindy is the real key for me on this cover, though. She joins the band from the right side of the frame, wearing a white dress and a matching beehive to compliment Kate's – but it's where she's located that I find the most interesting: popping out of a door. It's ironic that the only straight member of the band appears to be coming out of a closet.

If it was a signal that the B-52s were coming out of the closet, then, like so many of us taking those first tentative steps, the band was getting ready to make some very bad decisions in the wake of their announcement. For me, those decisions were still a few decades away: bad boyfriends, hopeless crushes, and waking up with regret. For the Bs, well, let's investigate some of the bad choices the band made on the other side of that closet door!

When I first spotted *Party Mix!* at a local record store, I gasped in delight; I had no idea the band had a new record. I immediately grabbed it, flipped it over, and was confused then sorely disappointed, to see six song names that I already knew well. I didn't know what a 'Party Remix' was, but despite my disappointment, there was no way I wasn't taking that cover and this new record home with me.

The B-52s were ahead of the curve in releasing alternate cuts of some of their more popular tunes on *Party Mix!* Record stores would soon be flooded with 12-inch singles containing extended and alternate mixes of hot tracks from all sorts of bands. These mixes were primarily intended for dance clubs and DJs, but the record industry sniffed a profit opportunity and mass-marketed the hell out of those things. The B-52s' was the first alternate mix record I bought, and soon my record collection would be filled with extended mixes of Depeche Mode, Tears for Fears, The Cure, Thompson Twins, and more – those records were badges of honour amongst friends and fellow fans. Oddly, the B-52s didn't really follow suit with 12-inch singles for any of their future releases. It wouldn't be the last time the band seemed to miss out on a pop culture opportunity.

Several years later, *Party Mix!* would fuel many late-night dance parties with me and my straight crush Scott (speaking of bad choices – straight crushes!). Late nights drinking with friends would often end with the two of us in my living room, flailing away like madmen to these reworked tracks. *Party Mix!* was meant to make us fans dance, and boy, did it ever. Those late nights with Scott, I frugged and shimmied with a fury previously unknown to me; my misplaced lust for Scott was expressed in movement to my favourite band.

There weren't a ton of original ideas on *Party Mix!*, but it sure was a lot of fun. I still have the indelible green cover in a frame in my home. *Party Mix!* provided a lot of teenage joy, which was lacking in my life during those years; I love it for that reason alone.

The same month that *Party Mix!* was released, the *New York Times* reported on 3 July 1981 of a 'RARE CANCER SEEN IN 42 HOMOSEXUALS'. We all know how this story turns out, but it would be a few years before I – and I suspect many other B-52s fans at the time – would understand what this article was foreshadowing. I had a few more years of ignorant bliss ahead of me. The disease wasn't known as HIV/AIDS just yet, but the storm was coming.[1]

While the fans danced to *Party Mix!*, we waited. And we waited some more. Meanwhile, REO Speedwagon topped the charts with their *Hi Infidelity* album in 1981, and I made out with a few girls at basement parties. I wasn't sure I liked the kissing, and I would often be looking over my make-out partners' shoulders at the cuter boys I had stronger feelings for. But boys weren't allowed to kiss boys, were they? Then why did I like staring at Keith on that *Party Mix!* cover so darned much?

Those last few years of grade school in the early 1980s weren't all bullying and public shaming. It was also the time when I had my first gay friend, though I didn't realize it at the time. Jim was a year older and a grade higher than me, and that distinction in public school usually meant a social line that you couldn't cross. Our older brothers were friends, and maybe that was how we connected, but I think we saw something in each other that neither of us could define. When Jim was in grade eight, he took me to the newly opened Eaton Centre multiplex in Toronto to see a film he was a fan of: *The Rocky Horror Picture Show*. I had never heard of *Rocky*, but Jim prepped me in advance by playing the soundtrack (he had the film *and* the stage versions!) and told me when we would have to throw toast and put newspapers over our heads. I was confused by this interactivity, but when I saw it come to life, I fell in love. My prepubescent brain did not quite know what to make of Dr Frank-N-Furter, but I was wildly entertained and more than a little titillated by the good doctor's bustier, to say nothing of Rocky's gold lamé bikini!

Jim and I talked about our love for *Rocky Horror*, *Fame* – the film and the TV series – and *Grease*, but we knew to keep those affinities to ourselves. We also listened to music together, including the B-52s. During a visit to his family's vacation house outside the city, we wore towels on our heads emulating the amazing women of the Go-Go's as photographed on their debut record *Beauty and the Beat* as well as Cindy and Kate's beehive hairdos on the covers of the

B-52s' records. We danced and frolicked on the beach in our bathing suits and makeshift wigs, playing in the sand and the cold water of the lake. Two queer boys having the time of their lives, free from the eyes and the taunts of our classmates. I wish I had hundreds more memories like this one, but it's one of a kind. When I suggested we show his parents our new 'dos, he recoiled in horror and firmly refused. We were having a blast, but at Jim's reaction, I knew that what we were doing was wrong.

There was never a sexual charge to our friendship. I was still too young to understand what was happening. Jim went to high school and left me behind; it proved to be a permanent fork in the road of our friendship. My first gay friend. It would be many years before I had another.

*** *Mesopotamia* 1982 ***

1982's *Mesopotamia* is one of the great records that never quite was. The B-52s were looking to expand their sound and decided on David Byrne as the producer for their next album. Chris Frantz joked that firing the head of your record label as producer maybe wasn't the most politically astute decision, and Frantz is probably right on that point. That choice was potentially the start of the trouble for *Mesopotamia*.

The pairing of the B-52s with David Byrne should have resulted in one of the greatest new wave (or post-punk, or whatever you want to call it) records ever made. Instead, it's a bit of a mess. OK, a lot of a mess. There are a ton of great ideas and several good songs on the final release, but *Mesopotamia* just feels unfinished. More insulting to us fans, instead of a full album, we only got another six-song extended play. At least this was new material, but still, only six songs? I felt a little short-changed, and I know I wasn't the only one.

Can I blame David Byrne? I'm going to blame David Byrne. Byrne is a hero of mine and Talking Heads are one of the all-time great bands – go watch Jonathan Demme's *Stop Making Sense*, the greatest live music concert film ever made, if you need a minute to digest that. But still, I blame David Byrne. On paper, he was the perfect producer for the job; he had great musical sensibility but, more importantly, the Talking Heads and the B-52s had played on the same bill several times and even toured together. Byrne knew the Bs and their artistry very well.

It's important to keep in mind that the B-52s recorded *Mesopotamia* with Byrne in September of 1981 in New York City and the EP was released in January the following year. Let's look at what Byrne was up to in and around that time.

- Talking Heads released *Remain in Light* in October of 1980, and during the following year, the band released several singles and supported the album with live shows. Talking Heads was keeping Byrne very busy in 1981.
- The year 1981 also saw the release of two – yes, TWO – albums from Byrne outside of his work with Talking Heads: first his collaboration with Brian Eno, *My Life in the Bush of Ghosts* in February, and the second was a solo project, *The Catherine Wheel*, his score to a

Twyla Tharpe dance piece in December. December! Two months after the B-52s sessions!

- That's not all. He worked with his bandmates to produce the double live album release *The Name of This Band is Talking Heads* that came out in March of 1982. Two months after the release of *Mesopotamia*.
- Later in 1982, Byrne would record with Fun Boy Three, producing their second album *Waiting*, released in early 1983.

Given all of these demands, it's impossible to believe that he was giving his best self to the B-52s during the recording and/or mixing of *Mesopotamia*. What a shame. The combination of the Bs' absurdist humour and Byrne's off-beat sensibilities and love of a deep funk groove should have been a match made in heaven. The Bs would have likely been in better care with any of the other Talking Heads members. I would love to live in another world where Tina Weymouth and Chris Frantz worked their Tom Tom Club magic on *Mesopotamia*. Frantz would too. He admitted to me during our conversation that he was disappointed by the B-52s' choice of Byrne and would have loved to have been asked to produce the record alongside his wife. We can only dream about what that version of *Mesopotamia* might have sounded like.

Though they only had six tracks, a few of which still sounded kind of raw, I think the record company panicked and released *Mesopotamia* anyway. Kate shared this with AV Club in 2011 about *Mesopotamia*: 'we hadn't even finished. "Cake" wasn't really finished. "Deep Sleep," I just kind of stuck that lyric on in the studio in one take. It was just not finished. We sometimes think, "Wow, if only we could go back and finish Mesopotamia." [Laughs.]'[2]

Kate confirmed in a *Stereogum* interview that the band felt rushed making *Mesopotamia* but she also squashed a long-believed rumour that the band didn't like working with Byrne. Kate tells the website, 'I don't know how that rumour got started that it was acrimonious. It was a delight to me.'[3]

The band was decidedly out of its element recording *Mesopotamia*. The album was recorded in NYC, a first for the B-52s. In the wake of *Wild Planet*, they had bought a house in Mahopac, just north of New York, but it didn't turn out to be the utopian live/work space that the Bs likely envisioned. In 1990, Keith and Fred talked about that house and that time in *SPIN* magazine: 'It was a big house, we had plenty of room, but it was like we were in exile or something', says Keith. 'More like a low-security institution with five inmates', says Fred.[4]

Kate and Keith joke about the move in *Athens, GA: Inside/Out*, asking 'why did we ever leave?' They laugh about it, but I think there's some truth in that question. In Athens, the B-52s were part of a scene, and in upstate New York, they were a little lost. The Bs lived in that house during *Mesopotamia* and their next album *Whammy!* and I think some of that alienation bled through to those albums.

Released in January of 1982, *Mesopotamia* is not without its charms. What's missing is the urgency of the band's first two records. The wild abandon and the chaos. Keith's thrashing beats behind the drum kit are replaced with a wider palette of percussion and some smooth grooves with the addition of horns on a few tracks. While I applaud the band for trying something new, it all feels a bit muted. Or like Kate suggested, unfinished.

We don't even hear Fred on the record until song three, the title song, and even as a thirteen-year-old, I sensed that was intentional. I still wonder if Byrne and Schneider had differences in the studio.

The biggest surprise about *Mesopotamia* was the cover – where the fuck was the band? When I finally found *Mesopotamia* in a local record store, there was an illustration meant to suggest ancient hieroglyphics with five avatars to represent the band members, as well as icons of pottery, ankhs, animals, and musical instruments.

No disrespect to Desiree Rohr, who is credited with the illustrations on the sleeve, but I still can't really tell which drawing is supposed to represent which band member. Is that Fred on the left, and does he play trumpet now? Was that even a trumpet? I was confused. Fans were confused. Where were the real Cindy, Fred, Kate, Keith, and Ricky? Were they, or the record company, too uncertain of the project's appeal that they half-assed the cover?

When I pulled the record out of its sleeve, I was also surprised to see no sign of the instruction PLAY LOUD on *Mesopotamia*. Huh. Was I not supposed to play *Mesopotamia* loud? What kind of message was this?

And wait a minute, where was the queerness? *Mesopotamia* is the first hint of the band going a bit quiet on that front. There are no coded messages, no horniness. What's up with that? Had David Byrne de-sexed the B-52s somehow?

My favourite track on *Mesopotamia* is 'Cake'. I love the song's improvisational spirit and its chugging groove, but it would have been better served with a bit more mixing (pardon the pun). 'Cake' could sit with the best B-52s tracks of all time if it had had a little more time in the oven (sorry). Cindy and Kate still sell it, and boy, would I have loved to be at that recording session or at their table having a slice of that cake. It's funny, funky, and inspired but it's just not fully baked (the last pun, I promise).

MTV hit television airwaves 1 August 1981, the year before *Mesopotamia* came out, and it forever changed the music landscape. Suddenly, how a band looked became as important – or arguably *more* important – than how a band sounded. A group like the B-52s should have flourished in this new medium, but where was the video for 'Mesopotamia' or 'Loveland?' It is still inconceivable to me that a band that had built a reputation for their wacky outfits and sky-high wigs didn't jump onto this new visual medium.

Would a fun video, or a better album cover, have helped make *Mesopotamia* a hit? Or broadened the B-52s' fanbase to help them sell their future records? We'll never know. One thing is certain though – the B-52s' record company and their management team should have waited until the band was happy with *Mesopotamia* before rushing it to market.

Now that the B-52s were famous, no one was throwing bricks at them anymore – they were cool, untouchable. I was decidedly not cool in 1981. Not only were the kids bullying me; there was a teacher at Courcelette Public School who decided to get in on the action too. Rather than being an educator and caregiver of children, this man, who looked a little too much like Fred on the cover of *Wild Planet*, chose to become a tormentor.

ParticipACTION was a Canada-wide programme to inspire kids to be more physically active. Mirroring the Olympics, every student was awarded a Gold, Silver, or Bronze patch depending on your lap times, reps, and commitment. I got none of those. When I was told to run a lap around the track, I leisurely walked. When instructed to do a standing long jump, I hopped off the starting block. It went on and on for weeks – I was a stubborn little kid, confused why the other kids made fun of me for doing gymnastics, or picked me last for baseball teams, or why they felt so free to call me a 'fag'. If none of them wanted me for sports, why should I play along? The teacher in question had observed all of this, and when it came time for the 'awards presentation' he decided to parade me, gleefully, in front of the entire student body and administration as the only recipient of a Participant badge in the entire school (the entire city, if I remember correctly). Instead of seeing a kid who was struggling to fit in and attempting to sit me down and talk to me, he delivered the lowest blow possible, punching downwards and joining the kids in the school yard by taunting me for not being man enough.

It didn't end there. This same teacher also entered me into a track and field event against other kids a grade higher and a year older. I was a tiny boy in grade seven, running against giants. This was clearly further punishment for refusing to conform. I stood on the starting line looking at boys, all at least a foot taller, and watched them fly ahead of me.

I have one nice memory from that indelible track meet. There was another boy who was in the same predicament as I was on that starting line, and we somehow knew to finish the race together, way behind the pack, and high-five each other on the other side of it. Queer communion.

That teacher was an asshole, and it seems insane to recount these stories now, but that was our society in the 1970s and 1980s. It was totally fine for a teacher not only to ignore the homophobic taunts and bullying of my classmates but to join in on the action, with no repercussions that I am aware of. My humiliation was school-sanctioned.

While I was being bullied and waiting for another B-52s record, in May of 1982 the *New York Times* published the first mention of GRID (Gay-Related Immune Deficiency), helping cement the idea in the North American public's mind that this new disease exclusively impacted gay men. Reports like this from New York and San Francisco often define the narratives around HIV/AIDS, especially the stories about gay men. But we do a disservice to all the victims by ignoring the wider global impact; AIDS has never been just a disease for gay men. But that's another story.

Thankfully, the GRID acronym would be short-lived: for the first time, the US Centers for Disease Control (CDC) used the term AIDS (acquired immunodeficiency syndrome) in 1982. Gay Men's Health Crisis (GMHC), the first community-based AIDS service organization, was founded in New York City in 1982 too. The gay community was recognizing the need for community response and action since they weren't seeing action anywhere else.[5]

The need for community response was real. During a White House press conference in 1982, President Ronald Reagan's deputy press secretary Larry Speakes can be heard joking with attendees when asked if the White House is aware of the CDC's categorization of AIDS as an epidemic. Speakes and the attendees have a jolly old time laughing about AIDS and the 'gay plague'. The footage was brought to my attention while watching Laurie Lynd's excellent film *Killing Patient Zero* and I watched it in horror. *Vanity Fair*, *VOX*, *VICE*, and more have reported on it, and the audio footage is available on YouTube. It's shocking, and sadly, not surprising.[6] Even the White House thought gay men and AIDS were fodder for bullying and derision.[7]

No one was laughing when Michael Jackson released *Thriller* in 1982, forever changing the popular music landscape, but that album wasn't released until late in the year. Asia's self-titled debut was the number one seller in 1982. Soft rock continued to own the charts in the United States that year.

Mesopotamia was lost in the heat of that moment, and the wait for new B-52s music began anew.

*** *Whammy!* 1983 ***

The exclamation mark we first saw on a B-52s album on *Party Mix!* was back! Surely a good sign? Right?

The B-52s' fans had waited just shy of three years since *Wild Planet* for a proper full-length follow-up record, and we were hungry! Finally, on 27 April 1983, we got the album we'd been waiting for: *Whammy!*

The band found themselves back in Nassau at Compass Point Studios with Steven Stanley taking over production duties. Stanley seems an odd choice given the direction the band was headed on *Whammy!* Stanley had worked with Tom Tom Club on their debut record, an album that was steeped in funk and groove. *Whammy!* leaned heavily on drum machine and synth sounds for the first time in the B-52s career – it is the least funky or groovy record that the B-52s had released. If they really wanted to make a cool synth-pop record, they should have hired someone from New Order, OMD, or Kraftwerk. A musician from one of those bands looking to branch out, or even one of their producers with expertise to help them incorporate the synth sounds they were hearing in their heads. I'm not sure Steven Stanley knew what to do with the B-52s and their new drum machine.

Still, *Whammy!* is half of a great album. Similar to *Mesopotamia*, it has a few killer highlights, but it doesn't feel quite fully baked. If the band had taken their time, or let's be honest, if the record company let the band take their time, there is a really strong record to be made from the best bits of *Mesopotamia* and *Whammy!* In fact, the band had written three songs during the *Mesopotamia* sessions that they didn't have time to finish: 'Butterbean', 'Big Bird', and 'Queen of Las Vegas' that would find a home on *Whammy!*[8]

As always, my relationship with *Whammy!* started on the bus ride home from the record store with a close inspection of the cover. It was great to see the band in a full-colour photograph again but . . . flat wigs!?!? C'mon Kate and Cindy! Where are the trademark beehives the band was named after? What were fans to think of this development? The black background is another hint that maybe the B-52s were in their dark period. Is it snowing in this cover scene, or is that cocaine falling from above? What's that dog up to? And if Fido is lapping up the coke, he's in for a hell of a ride! What are they looking up into the sky for? A UFO to take them on another adventure?

Art direction choices aside, it was great to see the band on the cover of an album again after the illustrated *Mesopotamia*. Here the Bs were in their full technicolour glory. Sadly, it would be the last album cover to feature the band as a fivesome.

Reading the liner notes, I was puzzled to see that Keith and Ricky were credited with playing all the instruments, outside of the horn parts on 'Big Bird'. That felt a bit odd. It didn't feel very democratic and seemed to work against the B-52s' *anything-goes* ethos.

Whammy! starts out strong. With lyrics by Robert Waldrop 'Legal Tender' is a killer track, but what was that drum machine doing there? In a podcast with the B-52s touring soundman Frank Gallagher recorded during the COVID-19 lockdown, Kate joked that the drum machine sounded like a toy. It's the Achilles heel of *Whammy!* in my humble opinion.

Keith's driving drumbeat was the backbone of *The B-52's* and *Wild Planet*, as well as the band's frenetic live shows and, while he's credited with drums on the liner notes from *Whammy!*, that new drum machine is the dominant percussion sound we hear throughout the album. I'm not the only one who has noted Keith's drumming talent. *Rolling*

Stone stated in a 1980 feature article that Keith's drumming was 'propulsive' and 'has wisely been given a dominant place in the group's live sound mix'.[9]

Chris Frantz also commented to me that he was a huge fan of Keith's drumming and was disappointed when he stepped out from behind the kit. That backbeat was a key feature of the B-52s sound, and the drum machine was a pale substitute.

While *Whammy!* is not a perfect album, it's a much stronger effort than *Mesopotamia*, and the good news for the queers was that the hints at otherness were back. Not as overtly or as frequently as on *Wild Planet*, but it was a move in the right direction.

'Legal Tender' – While ostensibly a song about counterfeiting money, the real desire expressed in this song is to live outside the mainstream, outside of the need for a job or money. Waldrop's lyrics are clearly looking for a way out of the capitalist norms most of us adhere to.

'Song for a Future Generation' – Is there anything more queer than singing about your astrological sign? The best part of this tune is hearing Keith and Ricky take lead vocals for their verses – a first for the two shyest members of the B-52s.

Exploring the cave of the unknown huh Fred?

'Don't Worry' – Inspired by Yoko Ono's 'Don't Worry Kyoko (Mummy's Only Looking for Her Hand in the Snow)', the B-52s' reworking is a sweet nod to a favourite artist. I don't think there is a single vocalist who Cindy and Kate are indebted to more, best evidenced on 'Rock Lobster'. And 'Don't Worry' is a blast! While she got credit as the lyricist on the track, I guess they forgot to get permission from Ono or her record company? The Bs had to strip 'Don't Worry' from later pressings, but I'm fortunate enough that I bought a copy of *Whammy!* upon its initial release with the song intact.

Any band covering a Yoko Ono tune in the 1980s (OK, any era) is a defiantly queer act, but *Whammy!* could have used a bit more queer subtext. I want a whammy kiss to be an Urban Dictionary reference to rimming, but I think even for me, that's a stretch!

On the pop charts in 1983, English bands like Duran Duran, Eurythmics, and Culture Club were riding high, and Michael Jackson dominated everything with *Thriller* and its many smash singles – especially on MTV. Those bands spent small fortunes on their video clips, and while the B-52s finally joined the video age and made promotional clips for 'Legal Tender' and 'Song for a Future Generation', they were fairly low-budget affairs. All of a sudden, the B-52s wigs and outfits didn't look so radical or colourful. The culture they helped build had eclipsed them, and *Whammy!* only climbed to #29 on the Billboard album charts. Not a bad showing, but not the performance I'm sure the record company and the band were hoping for.

Cyndi Lauper's first single, 'Girls Just Want to Have Fun', was also released in 1983, and Cyndi is a perfect example of an artist taking the B-52s candy-coloured, thrift store chic to the top of the charts. The Bs had set the table for that kind of commercial breakthrough but somehow missed the meal.

The year 1983 saw the mainstream media and popular culture start to really pay attention to AIDS. The first *New York Times* cover story appeared on 25 May with the headline 'Health Chief Calls AIDS Battle "No. 1 Priority"'. *Newsweek* magazine was close behind with a cover story of their own, 'Gay America: Sex, Politics, and the Impact of AIDS'.

Near the end of 1983, the World Health Organization held its first meeting focussing on the global impact of AIDS. The medical community was realizing the devastating potential of HIV, even if the politicians didn't seem yet to care.[10]

In the world of comedy, Eddie Murphy released his first stand-up special on HBO in October of 1983, only a few months after the B-52s released *Whammy! Eddie Murphy Delirious* was incredibly popular and was noteworthy at the time because of Murphy's prolific use of profanity and his use of 'faggot'. Murphy didn't stop there; he thought AIDS was fodder for stand-up too and included some misinformed 'jokes' about getting AIDS from kissing your girlfriend who might have kissed a homosexual. What a laugh riot.

I don't raise the special to drag his name through the mud one more time (Murphy has since apologized) but more to highlight how normal it was to laugh at faggots and AIDS casualties. You can only imagine the vitriol I heard in the schoolyard and in the halls between classes; Murphy could have learnt a few things from my classmates.[11]

It wasn't the end of Murphy's trolling of the gay community. He'd continue to use the terms 'fag' and 'faggot' in the theatrical release of *Eddie Murphy Raw* in 1987. Neither his ignorance nor his homophobia had any impact on *Raw*'s success: it made over $50 million at the box office, still the highest-grossing stand-up comedy film of all time (as of this writing).[12]

As a young gay man, I heard Eddie's jokes, and those of my classmates, and internalized them all. It was cemented in my brain: gay men weren't just miscreants, they were dangerous too. AIDS was becoming part of the cultural conversation, but there was little nuance to the dialogue. In part, thanks to comedians like Murphy, I was positive that if someone was gay, they would get AIDS, and that if I was gay (and I was pretty sure I was), I was going to get AIDS too. Where exactly would that leave me?

I wasn't the only closeted gay man in the early 1980s internalizing these messages. I have talked with *a lot* of them.

The early 1980s were rough on me, but it wasn't all doom and gloom. Reading about Keith and Ricky playing music and making up songs in their teenage bedrooms reminded me of my friend Lorna and me taping ourselves on a portable cassette machine, playing recorders and singing alternate melodies to songs by the B-52s and Thompson Twins. Lorna and I also went on many shopping trips to the Goodwill 'Buy the Pound' store in Toronto to buy old 1960s and 1970s polyester outfits that cost us one dollar per pound: yes, they actually weighed your purchases on a giant scale, and we made out like bandits. Inspired by the B-52s, we would dress up in outrageous outfits, gender blind, and make wild and glorious noise. Unlike Keith and Ricky, who were using proper instruments in their teenage bedrooms, we banged away on whatever we could find.

I think we were fancying ourselves an extension of the band – the sixth and seventh B-52 members? The B-52s inspired creativity in me and I owe them a lot for that. Unlike the actual five members, though, I was still too afraid to show the world who I really was.

*** *Bouncing Off the Satellites* 1985–6 ***

I had hoped that *Whammy!* represented a return to form, or at least that the B-52s were back working full time, but it was time for fans to wait again. It would be another three years before the follow-up was released. Before the next B-52s record came to market, though, fans had some big news to process. Ricky was dead.

Ricky Wilson, founding member, guitarist, and some say heart of the band, died of complications from AIDS on 12 October 1985. He had completed work with the band recording, mixing, and mastering the next B-52s record, *Bouncing Off the Satellites*, but didn't live long enough to see its commercial release.

Ricky had decided to keep his illness mostly to himself, except for Keith. What a heavy burden that must have been on Ricky's friend and bandmate. Holding that knowledge while making an album with his best friend, and being unable to tell Cindy, Fred, or Kate what was going on with Ricky must have been brutal. Ricky's decision is emblematic of the times – HIV/AIDS was almost impossible to talk about with any sense of objectivity. His poor bandmates, including his sister, were left to wonder what was going on.

The B-52s were gutted by Ricky's loss, rightfully so, and decided not to tour in support of their fourth full-length record. The record company took this as a sign that the band was finished and did little to promote the album either.

Ricky's death was a bit of a mystery to the band's fans, including me. What happened? Where did he go? How did he die? These were a few of the many questions I was asking myself. Talking to T. Cole Rachel for *Pitchfork* many years later, Kate talked about the band's response, and the deplorable lack of curiosity of the press, to Ricky's death. 'We just didn't really talk about it publicly very much', says Pierson. 'That might have made people think we had some kind of shame about it or something, which was not the case. We just wanted to be respectful of Ricky's family – it was 1985. It was so different then. Literally no one ever asked us about it at the time.'[13]

This kind of silencing was completely normal for the time. Nobody wanted to talk about HIV/AIDS, and there were many obituaries written by family members of dead men that omitted any sign of queerness or mention of the true cause of their deaths. Dying of HIV/AIDS was seen as shameful.

By the time *Bouncing Off the Satellites* came out in 1986, the world had moved on from the B-52s, and so had I. *Bouncing Off the Satellites* was the first B-52s record that I didn't buy when it first came out. Seeing the Bs as a four-piece in the only video made to support the record, 'Girl from Ipanema Goes to Greenland', was strange for me and for all the fans. With no other videos, underperforming singles, and no tour, *Bouncing Off the Satellites* seemed to mark the end of the B-52s. It was the lowest charting record of their career, and they disappeared off the pop culture radar.

The year before, pop culture took a turn for the earnest. Live Aid, a bi-continental fundraising concert for Ethiopian famine relief, took place on 13 July 1985 – the world had seen nothing like it. Spearheaded by Bob Geldof and Midge Ure as a follow-up to their enormously successful 1984 single 'Do They Know it's Christmas', Live Aid was a once-in-a-lifetime concert event broadcast live from Wembley Stadium in London and John F. Kennedy Stadium in Philadelphia. It was the pop culture moment of the year, and I was glued to my television set along with millions all over the planet.

It's curious to me that the B-52s, the self-described 'World's Best Party Band', weren't invited to perform at the event. The Bs had proven to be favourites at massive festivals like Rock In Rio (January 1985), the Us Festival (September 1982), and at the Heatwave festival just north of Toronto (August 1980). Their absence at Live Aid is particularly curious. Weren't they invited? Was Ricky too sick to do it? Or maybe the B-52s style of heartfelt partying was too great a contrast to the solemness of the event? Was homophobia to blame? The organizers invited George Michael, Elton John, and Freddie Mercury (all still closeted in 1985) to perform, so . . . what was up? Whatever the reason, the Bs missed a massive opportunity to be seen and be part of the cultural conversation. Live Aid was such a big deal at the time.

The US response to Live Aid and 'Do They Know It's Christmas' was 'We Are the World'. Released in late 1985, the Bs might have dodged a bullet by missing out on that: it's a stinker of a tune, weighted down by its sense of self-importance.

Nonetheless, Live Aid and 'We Are the World', signalled a turn in the pop culture and pop music scenes. Earnestness and purpose, best exemplified by U2, were all of a sudden cultural currency. Bands had to *mean* something. Athens friends R.E.M. were much better suited to this climate. The B-52s were yesterday's news.

I finally bought a copy of *Bouncing Off the Satellites* in the early 2000s for two or three bucks in a used bin at a record store on Bloor Street in Toronto. I was in a long-term relationship that was not in great shape. Maybe I was looking for the comfort of old friends when I picked it up? I brought it home and had a visit with my old friends Cindy, Fred, Kate, Keith, and Ricky. Hearing *Bouncing Off the Satellites* truly for the first time, I was kind of dumbstruck. It was good. Great at times. Like many of the Bs projects in the 1980s, there's at least half a great album here.

To hear Fred talk about making the album to *SPIN* magazine, things didn't sound great in the B-52s camp. 'We had been together a long time, and we were still friends, but we had been falling apart a bit as a group', says Fred. 'We decided that everybody should write their own songs. I came up with "Juicy Jungle," Kate wrote "Housework."[14] It was also a different album in that it had more serious songs.' Fred elaborated in a *Rolling Stone* feature 'Everybody was doing their own songs because we were finding it harder and harder to jam and agree on things.'[15]

Tony Mansfield was chosen to produce *Bouncing Off the Satellites* and he's credited with playing the Fairlight synthesizer on every track. Was Tony a B-52 now? While Kate Bush's mastery of the Fairlight, an early sampling synthesizer, helped make *Hounds of Love* one of the all-time great albums, I'm not sure Mansfield's work is doing the same favour. *Rolling Stone* described *Bouncing Off the Satellites* as having a 'cold, mechanical sound' and I blame the Fairlight. It really cements the album in the mid-1980s.[16]

New wave contemporaries Devo also leaned heavily on the Fairlight for their 1984 album *Shout*. Looking back on his biggest regret of the band's career, founding member Gerald V. Casale told *Billboard*: 'Well, "Shout," because the Fairlight [synthesizer] just kind of took over everything on that record. I mean, I loved the songwriting and the ideas, but the Fairlight kind of really determined the sound.'[17]

Similar to *Whammy!*, Cindy, Fred, and Kate are relegated to vocals again and don't contribute musically except for Kate playing the organ on 'Housework', the track she wrote with Tim Rollins. Where did that B-52s camaraderie go? The *all for one* mentality?

For the first time in the Bs career, they were entirely absent from the cover. Even *Mesopotamia* had animated avatars, but not *Bouncing Off the Satellites*. I'm sure the record company had many discussions over what to do about a Ricky-less B-52s – nobody was ready to see the band as a foursome on the cover. Ultimately, they chose a painting by Kenny Scharf to grace the cover and, no offence to him, the visual has nothing to do with the B-52s or *Bouncing Off the Satellites*.

The most significant 'first' on *Bouncing Off the Satellites* wasn't the cover, though; it was the B-52s' first bummer track, 'Ain't It a Shame'. A song about the end of a relationship, thematically it's a bummer, but it's also one of the first Bs tracks that doesn't even try to get you on the dance floor. Maybe the mood of making *Bouncing Off the Satellites* and Ricky's mysterious behaviour bled into this song. It's a bummer track but a good one – it's a friend's favourite B-52s track, and it was his enthusiasm for it that really turned me onto it.

Somehow, I had missed Sinéad O'Connor's blazing cover of 'Ain't It a Shame' on her 2003 album *She Who Dwells in the Secret Place of the Most High Shall Abide Under the Shadow of the Almighty*. Maybe it was Sinéad's album title that put me off? Talk about two great things going great together! There are very few B-52s covers out there and none by major artists like Sinéad. It's an amazing compliment to the band and to Cindy's vocal performance.

What a shame that the band's final recording with Ricky went so unheralded at the time. Does it stand up to *Cosmic Thing*? No. However, there are some classic Bs' jams on this album. *Bouncing Off the Satellites* deserved better.

Chris Frantz described a memorial for Ricky in Brooklyn's Botanical Gardens where he had agreed to deliver a eulogy. Not an easy task. He was so emotionally distraught he couldn't get the words out, and no one else could either.[18] He told me it was one of his greatest life regrets. The B-52s and their community of friends were in shock. Following the memorial, there was a tree planting service to honour Ricky. Kate collaborated with Tina Weymouth and Tina's sister Laura to sing a classical song to say goodbye. Frantz lamented that the B-52s just 'sort of disappeared after that. Nobody heard anything from the Bs for quite a while'.[19]

Chris Frantz's emotion was genuine on our video call, and we both got a bit verklempt talking about Ricky's death and his memorial. His death had always felt sad to me, though it was removed from my life and experience. Talking with one of his close friends and sharing stories about his passing made it far more real for me. We talk of losing artists and icons to AIDS all the time, but seeing the real devastation on Ricky's friend really hit me in the gut.

The band members weren't sure they would continue. Keith told the *Daily Mail* about that period 'After Ricky died, we thought the band was finished because we couldn't imagine continuing without him.'[20]

The mid-1980s weren't just tough times for the B-52s; the entire gay community was suffering. Rock Hudson died in October of 1985, a week before Ricky. Hudson was the highest-profile AIDS-related death at the time, and it was his passing that really brought AIDS into mainstream. After Hudson died, Ronald Reagan finally acknowledged the disease and said the word 'AIDS' out loud. This was huge news at the time. Reagan was glacially slow to react to HIV/ AIDS, and his silence felt like a loaded gun aimed directly at the gay community.

The *LA Times* published the results of a poll in December of 1985 that found a majority of Americans supported the quarantine of people who have AIDS. Many gay people feared further discrimination against their community – there was talk in the schoolyard and on the street of concentration camps and segregated hospitals, driving those of us hiding on the sidelines further into the closet. It was not a pretty time.[21]

The year 1985 also saw the establishment of the Parents Music Resource Center (PMRC). Founded by a group of women, led by Tipper Gore, in response to what they believed to be objectionable lyrics and imagery in popular music. They identified the 'Filthy Fifteen' – songs too hot for Tipper and friends to handle. The list included pretty benign songs like Madonna's 'Dress You Up', Sheena Easton's 'Sugar Walls', and even Cyndi Lauper's 'She Bop'. Heaven forbid women talk about, or even suggest, sex and self-pleasure! We still have the PMRC to thank for warning labels on albums – though the sticker only served to make the targeted albums all the more enticing to the children Gore and her stable of Karens were ostensibly trying to protect.

Curiously, the PMRC didn't mind when Dire Straits used 'faggot' in their song 'Money For Nothing' from 1985. It seemed like Tipper and her friends wanted to silence any sexual expression, but homophobia was just fine.

I think the hysteria in the media about AIDS spelled the end of the party for fun in popular music, especially anything that might be a little bit 'gay'. For a few years in the early 1980s, when English imports like Frankie Goes to Hollywood, Duran Duran, Spandau Ballet, and Culture Club were ruling the airwaves, it seemed for a hot minute that gay was cool. It didn't matter if you actually were gay (Holly Johnson of Frankie Goes to Hollywood or Boy George) or not (all of Duran Duran and Spandau Ballet), but a whiff of gay was actually an asset. Not in 1985, it wasn't. The closet door got shut on pop music and it stayed that way for a long time.

In the wake of fey Brits, hair metal came to define masculinity as typified by the likes of Mötley Crüe, Def Leppard, and Bon Jovi. There were still loads of hairspray and make-up on those guys, but they were adamantly and stridently heterosexual. It was not pretty to watch, especially if you were a closeted homosexual teenager.

One singular artist towered above hair metal and everything else on the charts in 1986. Whitney Houston's self-titled debut album stormed pop culture and gave her the number one album that year. Whitney's bland pop was safe from the Parents Music Resource Center – if only Tipper and her friends knew Whitney had a girlfriend.

Amongst the rise of hair metal, the earnestness of U2, and Whitney dominating the charts, the Bs and *Bouncing Off the Satellites* never stood a chance. Like the love Cindy described in 'Ain't It a Shame', it seemed like the fuse of the B-52s career had burned out for good.

Notes

1 https://www.nytimes.com/1981/07/03/us/rare-cancer-seen-in-41-homosexuals.html

2 https://www.avclub.com/kate-pierson-of-the-b-52s-1798228355

3 https://www.stereogum.com/2244221/b52s-kate-pierson-career-spanning-interview/interviews/weve-got-a-file-on-you/

4 SPIN Magazine Vol. 5, No. 12, March 1990.

5 https://www.hiv.gov/hiv-basics/overview/history/hiv-and-aids-timeline#year-1982

6 Audio: https://www.google.com/search?q=white+house+audio+of+press+laughing+at+aids&oq=white+house+audio+of+press+laughing+at+aids&gs_lcrp=EgZjaHJvbWUyBgg

AEEUYOdIBCTEyMzgwajBqN6gCALACAA&sourceid=chrome&ie=UTF-8#fpstate=ive&vld=cid:592048b3,vid:yAzDn7tE1lU,st:0

7 https://www.slate.com/blogs/outward/2015/12/01/reagan_press_secretary_laughs_about_gay_people_dying_of_aids.html

8 https://www.rhino.com/article/deep-dive-the-b-52s-whammy

9 https://www.rollingstone.com/music/music-features/interview-the-b-52s-113100/

10 https://www.hiv.gov/hiv-basics/overview/history/hiv-and-aids-timeline#year-1983

11 https://www.thepinknews.com/2019/09/30/eddie-murphy-cringes-ignorant-old-jokes-aids-homosexuality/

12 https://www.boxofficemojo.com/genre/sg1591734529/

13 https://www.tcolerachel.com/b-52s

14 https://podcastaddict.com/soundman-confidential/episode/117014064

15 *Rolling Stone* 1990 Cover Issue

16 Ibid.

17 https://www.billboard.com/music/music-news/the-billboardcom-qa-devo-1055867/

18 https://podcastaddict.com/soundman-confidential/episode/117014064

19 Chris Frantz interview, Aug 22, 2024.

20 https://www.dailymail.co.uk/tvshowbiz/article-7242807/The-B-52s-guitarist-Keith-Strickland-reveals-tragic-death-nearly-ended-group.html

21 https://www.hiv.gov/hiv-basics/overview/history/hiv-and-aids-timeline#year-1986

4
'Cosmic Thing' 1989–90

Not only was the fuse not burned out, the B-52s were about to take flight again, reaching heights the band had never soared to.

In the aftermath of Ricky's death and the failure of *Bouncing Off the Satellites*, the B-52s weren't busy for the first time in a very long while. There was no tour to do, and the band did very little press and promotional appearances to support their last album with Ricky. No one expected a new album or single from the band, and there was no record label pressure.

So, they took time.

Time turned out to be the secret ingredient to success for the B-52s. There's a real and distinct pressure for a band to follow up a hit album with more – more hits, more albums, more shows . . . more of everything – mostly more money for the record company. Expectation can be the enemy of creativity, and I think the freedom from any pressures or expectations is what allowed the band to thrive during this next phase of their career.

While they had time, the fallout from *Bouncing Off the Satellites* also hit the B-52s' collective wallet. In a 1990 *Rolling Stone* article, Fred admitted: 'We were just barely staying afloat, living off our catalogue.'[1] The feature goes on to detail the band selling a variety of assets to help them stay solvent. A new record must have felt like a distant dream to the band, as much as it did to us fans.

Before the B-52s were even thinking about being together and making a new record, though, they simply needed to heal.

Cindy told *Yahoo Music* in 2023 about the time between Ricky's death and the making of *Cosmic Thing*: 'It was very depressing days. It was a dark time. It was just so awful with what was going on with the AIDS epidemic and so many lost loved ones and friends. We were all so depressed and didn't know what was going to happen', Cindy says. 'It seemed like the end of the world, really. It was really, really tough. But I felt better being with the band – with Fred, Kate, and Keith. It felt good to be with them.'[2]

Kate talked similarly about the difficulty of that period in their career in an online interview with *Celebrity Drop*: 'It was so devastating to lose Ricky and then so many friends after that. It was a really dark time.' Kate added: 'We lost a lot of friends . . . the whole community was devastated.'[3]

It's interesting to me that both Cindy and Kate use the term 'dark time'. It really was. When the B-52s recorded *Cosmic Thing* in 1988, AIDS was still rampant (effective treatment drugs wouldn't be readily available for several years), Reagan was nearing the end of his second term before handing the presidency to George Bush in 1989, in the UK Thatcher was *still* the prime minister, and in Canada we had a conservative government in power under Brian Mulroney. The late 1980s were truly dark times for queer people.

Losing friends and creative partners to an unpredictable disease was a story playing out in friend groups and artistic communities around the world in developed countries, never mind the devastation in Africa and the developing world. But dark times are when queer people find their strength. It's the dark times, when we're backed into a corner, that we come out swinging the hardest. Just ask Marsha P. Johnson, or any of the heroes of the Stonewall uprising. Instead of hiding their heads in the sand, or quietly fading out of the pop culture landscape and letting their catalogue languish in the remainder bins, the B-52s decided to go to work. Whether it was conscious or not, they resolved to fight through their grief and show the world that queer people would be visible, that they would dance, that they would sing, and in the face of tragedy, they would still find a way to smile and honour their friends.

After some rest and some healing, the B-52s still had a creative spark. Hearing the band talk about being together and creating art during that time demonstrates that making music was part of their healing process. *Cosmic Thing* started slowly, the creative ember starting to flicker.

Kate and Keith ended up with homes close to one another in Woodstock, New York. So close, in fact that they could canoe across a pond to visit each other. That's where *Cosmic Thing* started. Keith would play bits of music that he'd been writing for Kate, and I love to imagine them in the woods, or by a lake, playing the beginnings of what would be their next album.

Playing music can be therapeutic, and Cindy posited in *Rolling Stone* that working on *Cosmic Thing* was a kind of therapy for Keith. In a retrospective interview in 2018, she said 'I think Keith dealt with the shock by doing music every day. That was his way of getting over his depression.'[4]

The entire band talks in that same article about working together and healing in the wake of losing Ricky. They talk about trauma and liken their time together to a support group. The B-52s were really helping each other out of a pretty bleak situation.

'We came up from the very bottom on this one, we really did', said Cindy to *Rolling Stone* about the making of *Cosmic Thing*.[5]

Keith had written some great music, and Kate and Cindy both agreed to work as a band again. Keith recounted the next step. 'And then we called Fred and said, "Do you want to do it?" He said, "Sure."'[6]

The B-52s were a band again, and this time they were going to do it for the right reasons. Kate told *Stereogum* 'We made a promise: This was not going to be anything where we tried to make a hit. This would be from our hearts, we'd pour our souls into this.'[7]

The four bandmates took their work very seriously. They rented a rehearsal space in Manhattan and spent four days a week hard at work. Playing, rehearsing, and writing collectively for the first time in a long time.

Kate describes the band's process: 'Keith would write the instrumentation and we would jam on that. We'd all get together and pick out parts and paste them together, then we would learn the parts.'[8]

They spent a year working in that studio, and by the end of it, they had the outline for ten new songs. Cindy told *Rolling Stone* that 'it turned out to be such a healing thing to get back together again. It felt like Ricky was in the room'.[9]

The B-52s had done the work, they had the songs ready, and it was time to hit the studio. They didn't make *Cosmic Thing* alone though; the Bs built a superstar team to help them bring their vision to life.

The band had worked with Nile Rodgers on one track for the *Earth Girls Are Easy* film soundtrack, '(Shake That) Cosmic Thing'. The Bs were big fans of Nile and Chic and enjoyed working with him on the song, so he was a natural choice to produce *Cosmic Thing*. Nile was game, but his schedule wouldn't allow him to do the entire album. Enter Don Was. Don wasn't as well-known as a producer, but that would change very soon with his work on *Cosmic Thing* and Bonnie Raitt's massive comeback record *Nick of Time*.

Nile would end up producing six of the ten tracks on *Cosmic Thing* ('Cosmic Thing', 'Dry County', 'Deadbeat Club', 'Roam', 'Topaz', and 'Follow Your Bliss') with Don doing the honours on the other four ('Love Shack', 'Junebug', 'Bushfire', and 'Channel Z'). I like the fact that Nile and Don would both end up with a top three single out of working with the band!

Two super-producers, check. What would the B-52s look and sound like in a post-Ricky world?

When Ricky died, the record company was urging the band to hire a new guitar player, but the Bs weren't having it.

Keith decided to step into Ricky's very big shoes and act as the B-52s' lead guitarist. No easy task, but he had worked so closely with Ricky over the years, he was able to do the job seamlessly. No doubt with hours and hours of practice.

The B-52s dropped the Fairlight from *Bouncing Off the Satellites* and the drum machine from *Whammy!* and decided to flesh out their studio band to make *Cosmic Thing*. Sara Lee is the MVP of the new hires; she plays bass guitar on every track except for 'Channel Z' where no bass is credited. Do I still wish Keith did double duty and got behind the drum kit? Yes. But the session drummers they brought in, Steve Ferrone, Sonny Emory, Charley Drayton, and Leroy Clouden, all did fantastic work on the tracks they contributed to. It was lovely to hear real live drums again on a B-52s record.

Keyboard duties were shared amongst a few musicians, but Kate got back behind her keys for several tracks, and Fred was banging away on percussion too. The full band approach was back in action for the B-52s for the first time in a long time. The secret of their success was always teamwork, the contributions of everyone, and finally, they figured that out again. The Bs were truly a band again.

Cosmic Thing is really the first B-52s album of real songs. Front to back. They're not novelty tracks, they're not silly. There is real emotion. Real depth. Real tenderness. And a whole lot of horniness. *Cosmic Thing* is by far the B-52s' horniest record since *Wild Planet*. They're still the good old Bs – there are moments of humour and levity, and you can dance your ass off to *Cosmic Thing* but there was something new here. More artistry coupled with the wisdom of age and experience maybe? This was a band that had seen a lot in the time they had been together and they were ready to share a piece of themselves the world hadn't seen before.

We were still living in the analogue age in 1989, so my journey with *Cosmic Thing* began like all of the other B-52s albums before it: the cover. It has taken me thirty-five years, but finally, staring at the cover for hours while writing this book, I realized, it's a rainbow flag. The B-52s were waving a rainbow-fucking-flag at the world! How did I miss that? Maybe I was still too deep in the closet when it was released to notice the symbolism, but in retrospect, it's impossible to miss the message. The *Cosmic Thing* cover is like a gay pride flag (of the era), and while the band members still weren't out, they were flying a flag in our collective face saying, *look a bit closer, listen a bit closer*. I was still too scared to look or listen.

For the first time in the band's history, the B-52s are photographed on an album cover with their instruments. Kate and Cindy behind familiar keyboards and bongos respectively, Keith with the guitar (a bit of a shock for B-52s fans!), and Fred with a mic and tambourine. Pictured here is a band. A real band that plays real instruments. A subtle reminder that the Bs aren't a studio group or a manufactured confection. These four people were the artists responsible for the music. They write the songs; they play the instruments.

There is a bit of a filter on the photo of the B-52s, and maybe the colour treatment was to make it easier to see the Bs as a foursome. The gay-rainbow colour treatment is less stark than seeing a full-colour shot of a Ricky-less B-52s. Smart choice, design team.

What is a cosmic thing? I don't know, and I'm not sure I ever will, but like so many of the band's otherworldly song titles, *Cosmic Thing* suggests otherness. Something from a different place or space. Or a new way of thinking. *Cosmic Thing* would be like nothing else I had heard or that the band had transmitted before.

Now we can pull *Cosmic Thing* out of the shrink wrap and give it a good queer listen. While my first copy of the album was a CD, I've rectified that with the purchase of a few vinyl copies since, and that's the journey we're going on now, with two distinct sides.

Side one is a nostalgic look back into the B-52s' early days, becoming friends and forming a band.

Track 1: 'Cosmic Thing'

When Fred tells me to gyrate 'til I've had my fill, I hear only one thing: he's telling me to fuck. With abandon, like a pneumatic drill. This was not the message from anyone else. 1989 meant safe sex, or no sex. Fred and the Bs wanted us to get down and get nasty. 'Cosmic Thing' is a manifesto for the next forty-five minutes of music. Dancing. Fucking. Partying. Shaking that thing. With those first few words *Gyrate it till you had your fill*, I knew that the horny B-52s were back in the house. Is a *faux pearl ring* anything like a pearl necklace, Fred?

Don't let it rest on the president's desk – let's not lose sight of who the Bs were talking about. Ronald Reagan was still the president, in his second term, and the Bs, like so many of us, were likely dissatisfied with Reagan's response to HIV/AIDS. Don't let it rest indeed. If we wanted to change, it was up to us, not Reagan, not Thatcher, not Mulroney.

It's a frenetic and frantic song from the minute it bursts out of the gate. The B-52s were back with a vengeance. Shout out to Cindy and Kate on this track: can any band do 'whooos' like the B-52s?

Track 2: 'Dry County'

Musically, the song grooves along a gentle southern breeze, carried along by Kate and Cindy's incomparable harmonies. And wait, is that Fred singing, rather than his usual speak-shout delivery? His voice sounds quite lovely for a change. The song is steeped in nostalgia; an easy and sweet track celebrating the lazy early days of the band's friendship and starting the group.

A dry county is technically a booze-free zone, but when the Bs sing *what they want to do, they can't do* likely doesn't mean an alcoholic drink, but freedom of self-expression. Like so many who feel like we can't do what we want to when we're young and closeted, we need to break free from the 'Dry County' and shake off our youth to self-realize. The 'Dry County' is a lot like a 'Private Idaho' in this regard.

The Bs sing about feeling the blues a lot on this track and then throwing them out the door. Is this self-help instruction for the audience or advice to each other? Cindy, Fred, Kate, and Keith all had to shake off their own blues to be able to pull together and make *Cosmic Thing*.

While the song is nostalgic, their use of the present tense, *are here*, propels this song forward and out of the past. They're singing about having time. Time to hang out with your friends and just sit on a porch and swing. The scorching heat of the long, lazy days of summer. Remembering a time when they were a fivesome, not a foursome.

Track 3: 'Deadbeat Club'

This song is a great pairing with 'Dry County' and it too bounces along sweetly to Sara Lee's bassline.

Get a job? What for? I'm trying to think. Let's all welcome Keith back to vocals! It's his first vocal performance since 'Song for a Future Generation' and he sounds great!

We would talk every day for hours. Like 'Dry County' the Bs are reminiscing about having time. Time to chat and to hang out with your friends with very few cares in the world.

And man, do I want to dance in the garden in torn sheets in the rain with the B-52s. While I never did that exactly, I did have a lot of late-night skinny dips with friends growing up – when we were our own deadbeat club.

Like 'Dry County', 'Deadbeat Club' is loaded with nostalgia for simpler times. The Bs reference *25 cent beer*, a jukebox, and a local bar, Allen's, where they play '96 Tears'!

Wild boys and girls going out for a big time. Wasn't every time a 'big time' when we were all figuring ourselves out – straight or gay? My own 'big time' parties are burned in memory. The Bs crash parties and go to Normaltown (a real Athens neighbourhood!). They go skinny dipping in the moonlight. I want to hang out with these people. I desperately want to be a certified member of their 'Deadbeat Club'.

Oh no, here they come! Sounds like a warning for the straights to beware, the queer kids are coming . . . and nothing is stopping them.

Track 4: 'Love Shack'

This song jumps out of the gate with a banging beat paired with hand claps galore: Hello Motown! It's even got a horn part to die for! The B-52s had never sounded like this before, and Sara Lee's funky bass part is integral to the proceedings.

If the titular 'Love Shack' isn't a utopian queer space, well, I just don't know what the hell it's supposed to be. A place where we can simply *get together*. Sometimes that's all queers need, a space to call our own. *Glitter on the mattress* . . . there is glitter bloody everywhere according to Cindy, even on the highway! Who of us queer folk hasn't woken up to find glitter in our bed, or in my case, my chest hair, after a particularly fun night out at a gay bar or a Pride festival?

It's almost impossible to not love the funky little shack. That shared sense of community when you're on a jam-packed dance floor with your chosen family, new- or soon-to-be-lovers, kissing and grinding, the music pulsing through you, your friends so close you bump and sway together – it's transcendent. That's what the 'Love Shack' feels like. Don't let hearing it at your sister's wedding or at your nephew's bar mitvah ad nauseam spoil the song for you . . . 'Love Shack' is transcendently queer. Never forget it.

Track 5: 'Junebug'

Side one started in the stars and ends earthbound in the dirt and the mud with this classic B-52s jam. 'Junebug' holds a similar place that 'Wig', 'Butterbean', and 'Rock Lobster' do: it closes out side one of a B-52s album with a barn burner of a dance track. It's a full band rock out with Keith living out his guitar-god fantasies near the end.

While it may not be as obviously nostalgic as 'Dry County' and 'Deadbeat Club', the title alone suggests summer and heat and then bam, what a jam.

There are some great 'anything goes' vibes here – snakes, snappers, June bugs, alligators, and more cross-pollination of species, let alone gender fuckery! Everybody is getting down and getting nasty in this song, and it doesn't matter who they're getting their freak on with.

You know what I'm talking about? Yes, I think we do, Fred. With the following two lyric samples, we sure get the gist:

Well don't you listen to what they say, cause we're a little different anyway.

No prying eyes on a love celebration.

The Bs are spelling it out for us, not overtly, but pretty damn clearly. They *were* a little different, weren't they?

Time to flip the record. Side two is a look to a queer future, with a dose of nostalgia from side one.

Track 6: 'Roam'

Is 'Roam' about Ricky, about roaming in another plane? Hard to tell, but side two kicks off in the astral plane again.

Whether it's about loss and the afterlife or not, 'Roam' is definitely horny too.

Ride the arrow to the target one. Give me a break. *Take it hip to hip, Rocket through the wilderness*. What wilderness am I rocketing through when I'm hip to hip with another human? With lyrics from Robert Waldrop, who gave us 'Dirty Back Road', it's pretty easy to see the sexual innuendo throughout this entire song.

'Roam' also has a great guitar hook, thanks to Keith.

The listener gets a taste of queer visioning and is instructed to roam *without anything but the love we feel*.

The sexual innuendos just don't stop, and the Bs tell their audience to head *around the world, the trip begins with a kiss*. It's true, that first kiss with a member of the same sex is the start of a wild journey.

'Roam' is a near-perfect pop song, it's no wonder it was a big hit. I remember telling a friend 'Roam' was going to be even more popular than 'Love Shack'. I was wrong, but matching the number three slot that 'Love Shack' made it to sure ain't bad.

Track 7: 'Bushfire'

Tell us about the fire in your bush, Kate! We've got another horny tune on *Cosmic Thing*! There's something so beautiful about two women singing about orgasm, their bush fire, that delights me. We all know 'Lava' was about sex and orgasm and 'Bushfire' shares a similar vibe. With the instruction, *Hey everybody, bask in the afterglow*, the Bs are practically asking us to orgasm and share a cigarette in the post-sex glow. More songs about female pleasure, please!

'Bushfire' isn't only about female pleasure, though; Fred has a few thoughts on the fire in his bush. Fred's going to *hold back* . . . 'cause he doesn't want to get burned. Get burned by what, I can't help wonder – the HIV/AIDS virus that killed his friend, perchance?

Fred's *been lying here too long* and needs someone *to take me to the ground* but he holds back again. The inability to give into desire was a familiar one to me in the late 1980s and 1990s.

The landscape's burning red hot. No kidding Bs, sex and sexuality were red hot topics in 1988 when they recorded 'Bushfire' and while waving a gay flag on the cover was a symbolic gesture, 'Bushfire' is down and dirty at a time when sex was considered dangerous. The song ends with Fred shouting to be held – possibly a desire for the safest sex around.

Track 8: 'Channel Z'

The Bs get political, and they get it right this time. 'Juicy Jungle' on *Bouncing Off the Satellites* walked so that 'Channel Z' could run.

'Channel Z' details the horrors of impending environmental catastrophe, corrupt politicians, out-of-control consumerism, and falling stock markets – this was no sci-fi fantasy like 'Planet Claire'. The B-52s were drowning in all the noise, imagine if they wrote it today?

The Bs were warning us, and they were more than a little prophetic.

'Channel Z' doesn't just get stuck in all the noise, though; it looks towards a better future. There's something I love about Fred's constant pessimism throughout the song being met with Kate and Cindy's optimism.

I want the world to change. The Bs, or at least Cindy and Kate, were looking forward to a better future made by our actions and urged us to get on board. *We can make it happen*. To queer listeners, we knew that if we wanted to change, it was up to us to fight for equality and for an end to HIV/AIDS.

They never name AIDS, which feels like a bit of an oversight, but Fred does ask at one point where his umbrella is, a slang term for a condom. The language is there if we choose to find it.

'Channel Z' was a smart choice as a lead single. It deftly demonstrated that the Bs were back, they were on fire, and they were not to be messed with.

Track 9: 'Topaz'

'Topaz' takes us off the earth and beyond the stars to a queer utopia.

Topaz in nature is a mineral or gemstone, and on *Cosmic Thing*, 'Topaz' is one hell of a little gem. It's a beautiful and sparkling thing. Cindy and Kate's harmonies on this song are glorious.

While 'Roam' is about a trip, it's lustful and earthbound. 'Topaz' takes us on a journey to an imagined queer future. One with Ricky.

They B-52s ask us to take a trip *faster than the speed of love, through a tear in the clouds* and *up to heaven above.* Once we get there, they ask us to move *beyond the heavens above* and that *the universe is expanding.*

That's how future visioning works. How queer visioning works. We have to dream of a better place, a place where change is possible, and then it's up to us to get there. To make it happen.

The vocal layering of Kate and Cindy's harmonies near the end of the track is likely the most gorgeous they ever sounded on record together. It's a heavenly sound; singers and a band, finally working together after a few years of floundering.

Let's follow the B-52s and *walk in ecstasy.*

Track 10: 'Follow Your Bliss'

It's nice to have a chill-out track after such a wild ride.

Kate and Sara Lee are credited with vocals, but there are no discernible lyrics to be heard. 'Follow Your Bliss' grooves on a *Twin Peaks-y* guitar line from Keith – I think Angelo Badalamenti owes Keith a debt of gratitude for that sound!

'Follow Your Bliss' is the calm after the storm. Maybe everything is going to be alright after all? For the band? For queers? For all of us?

Maybe only if we did as the Bs instructed and followed our bliss.

OK, so *Cosmic Thing* was a banger from front to back. Would anyone notice? New Wave, the scene the B-52s were most often associated with, was all but dead in 1989. Many of the band's contemporaries had broken up – Blondie, the Go-Go's, the Cars – or were teetering on the edge of doing so – Talking Heads, Devo. The Bs were sort of the last band standing. The band had their work cut out for them, but like Lazarus, the B-52s were about to rise from the dead.

The band parted ways with their old manager, Gary Kurfirst, and hired a whole new team: new management, new accountants, and a new booking agency. The B-52s were looking to make a clean start. They even moved labels to Reprise, a subsidiary of Warner Bros. Records that championed smaller, independent bands. Oftentimes with great success.

Eventually, people would notice, but *Cosmic Thing* was a slow burn. The first two singles 'Channel Z' and 'Cosmic Thing' were well received on college and alternative radio, but for me, it felt like I was the only one listening to the new B-52s album. None of my friends were talking about the Bs, and the mainstream press and radio didn't seem to be all that interested either.

Then 'Love Shack' finally found its audience. While it sounded like an instant classic to me, the success of 'Love Shack' didn't come easily. Fred had to beg radio to play the song: 'I had to go with our A&R person, bless her heart, and beg radio stations to play it – they thought it was too weird. We felt "Love Shack" was probably the most accessible commercial thing we'd ever done, and finally they started playing it, and it made it all the way to No. 3 on the Billboard charts.'[10]

Fred's efforts clearly paid off. And once people started listening, for the first time in a long time, the critical reviews for a B-52s album were good.

SPIN magazine had this to say about *Cosmic Thing*: 'Sensitive, at times elegant, it's the first B-52's album where you don't need to get the joke.' Karen Schoemer went on to say: 'For a band long associated more with wild wigs and funny clothes than with serious music, Cosmic Thing comes as a watershed, a work of depth and emotion.' 'Throughout, the lyrics are more direct and descriptive, less humor-dependent than in the past. The words and the music speak louder than wigs and kitsch.'[11]

The B-52s had never been accused of *depth* or *emotion* in the press before. The tides had turned for my favourite little queer band.

The TV landscape had changed a great deal during the time since the B-52s' first record. They were invited back on *SNL* for the first time since 1980 and would also play on *The Arsenio Hall Show*, *Late Night with David Letterman*, and even headlined the MTV New Year's Eve show to close out 1989. Being chosen as the headliner for an MTV show would have been unthinkable at the outset of 1989, a meteoric rise for a band that was almost gone.

MTV finally loved the B-52s, and for the first time in their career, the Bs were able to take advantage of the video format to further their art. The clips from *Cosmic Thing* helped cement both their popularity and position them as queer icons.

'Channel Z' was the first video from the album, and the first images we see are of nature and then of the band playing alternately at a club and on a floating dock on a lake. Here the Bs' dualities are on display – hard-core rock and roll band and hard-core hippies.

The last image of the video is the four remaining members standing on the floating dock, reflected in a lake, looking towards something, away from the camera. Looking forward to a brighter future and leaving their past behind them.

The 'Love Shack' video came next, and it captured the spirit of the B-52s perfectly! A wild, colourful party where everyone is invited, the attendees are all dancing, and the band is having a blast.

To reinforce my theory that the 'Love Shack' is a queer space, RuPaul is featured in the video, dancing her heart out. There were not many mainstream bands in the top ten with drag queens in their videos in 1989, and having a Black drag artist in their video was a true radical act at the time. Ru would repay the favour many years later by featuring the Bs on *RuPaul's Drag Race*.

The 'Roam' video was the first one shot when the B-52s were bona fide rock stars. The band is dressed in all black, nothing particularly retro or kitschy, and everyone is obviously having a great time. Even Keith, who usually kept to the background, is seen barefoot and top-hatted, and, best of all, he's smiling, dancing, and finally having some fun. He also looks fantastic! Was Keith leaning into his heartthrob status?

Proof positive that 'Roam' is about insertive sex, there is an image of a banana penetrating the hole of a bagel at the exact time the band is singing *to the target one*. What else are we supposed to see here? It's around the two-minute mark that the most stark image appears: three guitars rotating on separate podiums, which I assume to be a tribute to Ricky. Are those three of his guitars, I wonder?

The final video from *Cosmic Thing* was for 'Deadbeat Club'. Again, the band looks like they're having so much fucking fun, like found footage of them having a party. Keith and Kate dancing is the most adorable thing, proof positive that these folks were still good friends. Keith in his black frame glasses is the perfect combo of sexy and sweet, and I love the shots of him mid-video lying down on the couch, smiling at the silliness of his friends. I think that shot captures so much about Keith and about this band. Keith has genuine pleasure in watching his friends fly. No jealousy, no ego. It's a decidedly queer approach.

It's not just Keith, though; the entire band looks so beautiful. A foursome of friends who stuck together and ended up successful and sexy . . . and they did it their way.

'Deadbeat Club' even features a cameo from Michael Stipe; all the cool – and quietly queer! – kids from Athens were there. Like the video for 'Channel Z', this one is equal parts party-time and nature-getaway. The sepia tone screams nostalgia, and they obviously want us to feel that sense of sentimentality while we watch and listen.

The video ends with another shot of them as a foursome, flipping through a magazine or coffee table book at the end of the party. Still together, facing the world. It's a gorgeous shot.

Now that the B-52s had a hit record and were beloved by the masses, they were selling truckloads of records and selling out shows wherever they played. For the first time in their career, the Bs were also nominated for two Grammys and four MTV Awards! The B-52s' career was in the stratosphere, right where they always belonged.

When *Cosmic Thing* was released, I was twenty years old. Twenty and still in the closet. I had barely eked out a high school diploma after five and half years of trying and had landed the most colourless job possible; I was a bank teller. In my mind, I still dreamed of being a wild and colourful member of the B-52s family, but I was dying a slow death of a thousand cuts by button-down shirts, casual Fridays, and customer line-ups amidst winding stanchions. I was sharing what was technically a one-bedroom apartment with one of my childhood friends, a B-52s concert poster proudly displayed on the wall across from my bed, in the unfinished basement. I may have still been in the closet, but I kept my friends the Bs close by.

It was my roommate Andrew whom I convinced to come and see the B-52s with me during their first leg of the *Cosmic Thing* tour in November of 1989. The gig at Superstars club in Mississauga was like a world away from our midtown apartment but with a bit of planning and a couch to crash on, we were ready. I assume Andrew's excitement was more muted than mine, but still, we were long-time fans and ready for a fun show.

My memories of the concert itself are a little clouded by time, I can really only pull up the image of the band on the *Cosmic Thing* cover as a visual. But the feelings are much more readily accessible. I had pretty much given up on ever seeing the band live, so just having the opportunity was a thrill. When the B-52s hit the stage, my little closeted brain exploded a bit. There they were: Cindy, Fred, Kate, and Keith in living technicolour flesh. I couldn't believe I was finally in the same room as my idols, my gay lodestars, and in my mind, my friends. I remember standing in the crowd, staring up at the empty stage in anticipation of seeing four of my guideposts in life, and the ghost of another, only a few feet from me.

Though 'Love Shack' was taking the world by storm when I watched that show, my fellow concertgoers were the devoted – the fans who coughed up the dough to see a beloved band months before their latest record became popular.

I got my first taste of queer joy that night. I couldn't name it and I didn't know it, but the feeling of community and camaraderie in the crowd as fans partook in a baptism by the B-52s was intense. We danced, we sang, and some of us – including me – even cried a little bit. Now that I'd had my first taste of queer joy, maybe I was ready to come out and admit to the world I was gay? Soon, but not so fast. I was still struggling.

The years 1989 and 1990 weren't just full of sunshine, B-52s joy and love shacks. In the same issue of *SPIN* that featured the B-52s on the cover, there was also a feature article on page 68 titled: *AIDS Spring Break: Sun, Sand, Sex. In the morass of dogma on safer sex, what you really need to know about AIDS*. B. D. Cohen, credited at the end of the feature as a 'Pulitzer Prize-winning science writer with Newsday' goes on to detail the relatively low risk of infection for white heterosexuals but includes this horrifying claim: 'In some cities, it is estimated that more than 70 percent of the gay population is HIV positive.' There is no source or reference to this statistic, but I assumed that if the Pulitzer Prize-winning science writer said so, he was probably right (and he probably was). Moreover, I assumed that Toronto was one of the cities referenced. Is it any wonder I was scared to go to a gay bar, let alone have sex with anyone who identified as gay?[12]

Cosmic Thing made it as high as number four on the Billboard Album Chart the week of 10 March 1990. The B-52s were kept from the top position by a curious trio of artists: Paula Abdul, Janet Jackson, and Phil Collins. Emblematic of the times. Just below the Bs, at number five, was Milli Vanilli.[13]

How they carved a path between Phil Collins and Milli Vanilli is anyone's guess, but 1990 was an ugly time for popular music. The top twenty that week also included the easy stylings of Michael Bolton and Kenny G, the hair metal of Skid Row and Mötley Crüe, and old stalwarts Aerosmith, Billy Joel, and Tom Petty. M. C. Hammer also debuted in the top 100 that week – Hammer Time was coming. New wave and no-wave were ancient history, and none of the B-52s' CBGB friends and peers were anywhere near the charts. The B-52s waving their technicolour weirdo flag at the time was akin to a revolution – yet somehow the Bs found a way to the top. *Cosmic Thing* was a little queer miracle.

An ugly time for pop music and a brutal time for queers. A few months before *Cosmic Thing* was released comedian Sam Kinison appeared on the cover of *Rolling Stone* in February of 1989. Kinison was vile, and his jokes make Eddie Murphy seem like a kindly old uncle making slightly off-colour remarks. In the accompanying article, Kinison addressed the controversy over his song 'Rubber Love' featured on his 1988

Grammy-nominated and certified Gold selling album *Have You Seen Me Lately?* Kinison is quoted in the article talking about AIDS and safe sex: 'GET OFF OUR BACK! Because a few fags fucked some monkeys . . . because of this shit, they want us to wear rubbers . . . "Heterosexuals die of it, too." Name ONE! It's not our dance.'[14]

As if that's not enough, the magazine quotes from Kinison's live show defending his AIDS joke: 'Nothing to start a fucking fag war over', and goes on to say to the audience 'Aren't you the same guys that tape up gerbils and shove them up your ass?' Hard to believe that a comedian that vile could sell half a million units of a comedy album and secure a *Rolling Stone* cover. Kinison would be dead a few years later in a car crash.[15]

It wasn't just Kinison who grabbed the baton from Eddie Murphy in the homophobia relay. In 1990, Andrew Dice Clay was chosen to host *Saturday Night Live*, which prompted a boycott from musical guest Sinéad O'Connor and cast member Nora Dunn, citing the sexism and homophobia in his act – and they were right to take a stand. Allies were starting to be heard and seen, but for the majority of the population, it was still fun to laugh and make jokes about gay people.[16]

While Kinison and Clay were making jokes, people were dying. Disco singer and queer legend Sylvester died in 1988 of complications from AIDS and out photographer Robert Mapplethorpe followed suit a year later. Sylvester's star had faded by the time of his death, but Mapplethorpe's final touring show, *The Perfect Moment*, caused quite a stir before his passing. The show was called out for being obscene and, because its organizers had received funding from the National Endowment of the Arts, the exhibit raised plenty of conservative eyebrows. Members of the US Congress and the American Family Association publicly opposed the exhibit, leading to its eventual cancellation. While the B-52s were flying high, more obvious queer artists, like Mapplethorpe, were still being silenced.

Queers were starting to tell their own AIDS stories in the face of ignorance and homophobia. The year 1989 saw the first screenings of an important film in the gay canon – *Longtime Companion*. Starring Bruce Davison, Campbell Scott, Mary-Louise Parker, and many others, it's one of the first feature films to address the AIDS epidemic and its fallout head-on. Spoiler alert: almost everyone dies. The film and its writer Craig Lucas weren't being dramatic, that's just how it was in 1989. A diagnosis still meant almost certain death. Watching the film when it came out on VHS, alone in hiding, did not dispel my worries about gay sex. But finally, gay men were being represented on screen. It wasn't breaking box office records at the mall multiplex, but the film was there, it could be seen.

Though the Bs were still not publicly out as queer, the band was giving us some pretty strongly worded hints. Kate had this to say in the band's *Rolling Stone* cover story:

> We have always appealed to people outside of the mainstream . . . Constantly we get people coming up to us and saying 'I was just the freakiest one in high school,

> I was the only one who kept playing the B-52's.' I think more people feel like they're outside of the mainstream these days – there's more people who are doing their own thing, feeling that it's not bad to be a weirdo and respecting other people's differences. And all that kind of goes into the big ol' B-52's philosophy.[17]

Reading Kate's words now the subtext is clear, but I would have loved the writer to ask a few more questions about exactly what 'outside the mainstream' and 'other people's differences' meant.

While the Bs were flying high, the pandemic was still raging. Reported cases of AIDS in the United States reached 100,000 in 1989. That is a lot of people, and a lot of loss.[18]

Yet, amidst all of this silencing, the death and disease, and the mourning, the B-52s threw a rainbow-coloured queer party with *Cosmic Thing*. Bless them for that.

The Bs were reborn. What new heights would they reach after *Cosmic Thing*?

Notes

1 https://www.rollingstone.com/music/music-features/interview-the-b-52s-113100/2/

2 https://www.yahoo.com/entertainment/b-52s-cindy-wilson-solo-album-triumph-after-tragedy-215747110.html?guccounter=1&guce_referrer=aHR0cHM6Ly93d3cuZ29vZ2xlLmNvbS8&guce_referrer_sig=AQAAALzptuAFq9AhicvvY0Yvm0qM4PP0fL8GRpkTlaIWWFjizkaxCkRL2FRI_Ems290jGga3Th-8WLtnO-P9RfMtjjysPEGP1Exz-WTk

yNR2epqKPuXrsL7EhEjv7fywjJYOSM3TzOifktsD9wrtml_RsPzVqCHFgI-2rvLs-WcULtPZ

3 https://www.youtube.com/watch?v=xKiwSeZR5_4

4 https://www.rollingstone.com/feature/love-shacks-rock-lobsters-and-nude-parties-the-b-52s-in-their-own-words-627925/

5 https://www.rollingstone.com/music/music-news/the-b-52s-mission-accomplished-231021/4/

6 https://www.rollingstone.com/feature/love-shacks-rock-lobsters-and-nude-parties-the-b-52s-in-their-own-words-627925/

7 https://www.stereogum.com/2244221/b52s-kate-pierson-career-spanning-interview/interviews/weve-got-a-file-on-you/

8 https://www.rollingstone.com/feature/love-shacks-rock-lobsters-and-nude-parties-the-b-52s-in-their-own-words-627925/

9 https://www.rollingstone.com/feature/love-shacks-rock-lobsters-and-nude-parties-the-b-52s-in-their-own-words-627925/

10 https://ew.com/music/b-52s-stories-behind-hit-songs/

11 *SPIN* Magazine, cover profile, March 1990

12 *SPIN* Magazine, Vol. 5, No. 12, March 1990

13 https://www.billboard.com/charts/billboard-200/1990-03-10/

14 https://www.rollingstone.com/culture/culture-news/the-devil-and-sam-kinison-63844/

15 https://www.rollingstone.com/culture/culture-news/the-devil-and-sam-kinison-63844/

16 https://www.esquire.com/entertainment/tv/news/a43718/andrew-dice-clay-showtime-dice/

17 https://www.rollingstone.com/music/music-news/the-b-52s-mission-accomplished-231021/3/

18 https://www.hiv.gov/hiv-basics/overview/history/hiv-and-aids-timeline#year-1990

5
'Keep This Party Going' 1990–2025

It's hard watching your heroes struggle. Following the B-52s' career in the aftermath of their *Cosmic Thing* triumph was tough for me. The success the band enjoyed thanks to *Cosmic Thing* was unparalleled in their career. The record sales were astronomical, the chart positions were the highest the Bs had ever hit, and outside of giant festival gigs, they were playing to the biggest audiences of their lives.

The downside of all that success was the expectation. That's the vicious cycle of the music industry, which mirrors the vicious cycle of consumerism and capitalism. The B-52s were red hot, and everybody wanted more.

Kate was the breakout star of the band in the very early 1990s with a few guest spots on the B-52s' peers' records. It was the first time the band's fans saw one of the B-52s leave the fold. Fred had released a record in 1984 under the Fred Schneider and the Shake Society moniker, but it didn't make much of a dent in the charts or on MTV; honestly, nobody really noticed. Including me. While Kate guested on Fred's

1984 album, it wasn't until the early 1990s that she gained real notoriety as a guest singer.

First came the single 'Candy' with Iggy Pop from his *Brick by Brick* album in 1990. It's a banger of a tune, and I suspect, like many, I bought *Brick by Brick* because of 'Candy' and Kate's participation. The song is a classic duet; a story of lost love told from two different perspectives. In the video, we see Kate as a femme fatale in a long blue cocktail dress at a bar, belting out 'Candy' like a torch singer in a jazz club – all the while Iggy, right on brand, is shirtless the whole video. Kate looks and sounds incredible. Produced by the B-52s' new friend Don Was, 'Candy' was the biggest hit of Iggy's storied career, cracking the Billboard Top 30 for the first and only time. While 'Candy' was a big hit, the real pop culture juggernaut was still to come for Kate.

Athens friends R.E.M. released their breakout album *Out of Time* in 1991. The first single from that album 'Losing My Religion' was a smash, but it was the follow-up single where B-52s fans got to really see, and hear, Kate shine: 'Shiny Happy People'. R.E.M. are still criticized for that song but in my book any track that gets you an appearance on Sesame Street, singing 'Furry Happy Monsters', is your masterwork. It's a shame Kate wasn't part of R.E.M.'s appearance on Sesame Street, but to inspire a purple Muppet in a red dress and wig has to be one of life's great compliments.

Kate sang on two other tracks on *Out of Time* – 'Near Wild Heaven' (another single release) and 'Me In Honey'. She and Michael Stipe sound incredible together, her voice blending with his and the guitar-driven sounds of R.E.M. seamlessly. I wish Kate and R.E.M. had done it again. Can I please request a Kate Pierson and Michael Stipe side project, please? It's not too late.

Like many fans, Kate's success with Iggy Pop and R.E.M. and her resulting increased visibility in the pop culture landscape made me think that she was the real powerhouse vocalist in the B-52s, that she was irreplaceable. But like any great team, we would see, all the members were equally important.

Kate was the most visible B-52 during this time; however, it was Cindy who would truly rock the Bs' fan base, and no doubt the band. After the gruelling worldwide tour and promotion of *Cosmic Thing*, Cindy decided it was time to hang up her wig for a while. She wanted to rest, and she wanted to have a kid; neither goal was a real possibility while on the road. Recording a new album and heading out on another endless world tour was not in the cards for Cindy Wilson, so she gave her notice and took a break. I have huge respect for her in making that choice. And honestly, I wish the rest of the band had taken her lead and followed suit to take some time to breathe and recharge creatively.

But Fred, Kate, and Keith soldiered on as a trio. For the first time in the band's history, the B-52s were Wilson-less.

*** *Good Stuff* – 1992 ***

As the band began to work on the follow-up to *Cosmic Thing*, they were in a similar place as they were ten years before, in the wake of their first two successful records. The band was red hot, they had momentum and buzz going for them but on the flip side, they were also really tired, which is not a great place to be when needing to be creative.

Keith admitted as much in a *Rolling Stone* interview looking back at that time in the band's career. 'We were burnt out from so much touring but we had to write another album quickly', he said. 'Our manager at the time pushed us.'[1]

Keith also admitted to trying to recreate the success of *Cosmic Thing* during the writing and recording of the new album, *Good Stuff*. Instead of writing for themselves and having fun like the Bs did for *Cosmic Thing*, they were thinking about chart positions and album sales instead. The B-52s were rushed, and the work suffered. Just like the band's work following 1980's *Wild Planet*, things went a bit awry.

Good Stuff was released in 1992 and it joined the *half-a-good-B-52s-album* club, a far less illustrious one than the club full of deadbeats. Like *Mesopotamia*, *Whammy!*, and *Bouncing Off the Satellites* before it, *Good Stuff* has its share of good ideas and great songs, but as Keith alluded, they just weren't ready to make another album.

Despite having super-producers Rodgers and Was back on board, Cindy's absence is felt deeply. Both producers layered multiple tracks of Kate's vocals on top of one another in an attempt to recreate something akin to those Kate and Cindy vocal harmonies. It just wasn't the same.

The sad thing about all of it is that Kate's vocals had never sounded better on record. She simply sounds amazing! All of that touring and rehearsing, and the confidence that must have come from the success of *Cosmic Thing* and her hits with Iggy Pop and R.E.M. all paid off. I think the best vocals of Kate's career are found on *Good Stuff*. Great-sounding vocals or not, the songs themselves were lacking. And the undefinable magic of the Kate and Cindy harmonies was gone.

The marketing of the record was confusing too. I understand why the record label chose 'Good Stuff' as the lead single – it felt akin to 'Love Shack', or at least one of the zany B-52s songs the band was famous for. The video for the song features a smorgasbord of partygoers and extras, not so dissimilar to 'Love Shack' which they were obviously trying to recreate. It's a whole lot of visual noise to make up for the lack of one Cindy Wilson. 'Good Stuff' cracked the top thirty – not the same heights as 'Love Shack' or 'Roam', but a respectable performance.

The next choice in singles is a real head scratcher. 'Revolution Earth' is without a doubt the best song on the album, another track with lyrics by Robert Waldrop, but it was overlooked. I think the label expected other songs to hit the charts harder because they would hold 'Revolution Earth' as the fourth single. By then, it was too late.

Instead of 'Revolution Earth', the second single from *Good Stuff* was 'Is That You Mo-Dean'. 'Mo-Dean' is one of the weakest tracks on the entire record, and despite the outer space lyrical content the Bs are well known for, I can't imagine who chose this as a single at all. The video for 'Mo-Dean' features individual shots of Fred, Kate, and Keith – separate but trying to make a music video or the appearance of a band working well together. Perhaps a fitting metaphor for where the band was at during this time – apart. The lone bright spot is seeing Julee Cruise!

Ahh . . . Julee Cruise. The B-52s realized they needed a second female voice for touring, and Julee Cruise got the nod. She had just enjoyed her most successful work courtesy of Angelo Badalamenti and the soundtrack to *Twin Peaks*. No one was expecting the dulcet tones of Cruise and her low-fi, ambient records to fit in as a B-52, but she turned out to be the perfect choice; she really let loose with the B-52s and found her inner party girl.

Julee Cruise loved working with the B-52s, and perhaps, that's the greatest legacy the band leaves behind from those times. When Cruise died in 2022, her partner Edward Grinnan wrote in a social media post that her time with the B-52s was 'the happiest time of her performing life'. Grinnan further elaborated: 'She will be forever grateful to them. When she first stepped up to the mic with Fred [Schneider] and Kate she said it was like joining the Beatles. She will love them always and never forget their travels together around the world.' Grinnan even played 'Roam' during Julee's transition from living to another dimension.[2]

But Cruise wasn't the only substitute for Cindy Wilson. One memorable night in March of 1992, Oscar-winning actor Kim Basinger filled Cindy's formidable shoes and did a pretty good job of it too. The performance is available on YouTube if you don't believe me!

While the album and the singles may not have performed to the expectations of the label or of the band, the B-52s were still riding high on the fumes from *Cosmic Thing*, and they toured the hell out of *Good Stuff*. Even if record sales weren't up to expectations, the fans continued to show up at the band's gigs.

Interestingly, *Good Stuff* is the only B-52s album made exclusively by queer members of the band. While gay culture was still mostly silenced in 1992, what a wild ride *Good Stuff* might have been if Fred, Kate, and Keith went all the way queer on this one! The sexiness of *Cosmic Thing* is entirely missing on *Good Stuff*, even with Fred singing about a 'Hot Pants Explosion'. The whole project just felt forced.

Side note to Nile Rodgers: why on earth did you let 'Dreamland' go on for over seven and a half minutes? If there was ever a B-52s song that needed a good edit, 'Dreamland' is the one. Skip.

The Bs still got a Grammy nod for Best Alternative Album for *Good Stuff*. It's telling that the band had been demoted to the 'Alternative' category after the chart-topping smash of *Cosmic Thing*. That must have been a bit deflating for the group. The B-52s' grip on mainstream success was slipping.

Pop culture and the record-buying public had moved on to different artists. In 1992, the number one position on the Billboard album charts was either Garth Brooks or Billy Ray Cyrus for thirty-four out of fifty-two weeks. Yikes. Clearly, the record-buying public was not ready for *Good Stuff*, or good stuff for that matter.

The reviewers were not kind to the album, which surely didn't help its fate. *Entertainment Weekly* said at the time that 'The B-52's are too smart to reduce themselves to self-parody, but their attempts to keep the party going on *Good Stuff* sound more forced than ever.' The review also suggested that 'A B-52's Saturday-morning cartoon show didn't seem too far off.' Ouch.[3]

That cartoon was soon to come.

I had recently turned twenty-three when *Good Stuff* was released, and while I was mostly out of the closet (just not to my family yet), I was too terrified to be sexual. Nor did I put myself in situations that might result in a sexual opportunity. AIDS became the number one cause of death for men aged twenty-five to forty-four in 1992, and the news about HIV/AIDS was still exclusively bad.[4]

When I would summon up the nerve to enter a gay bar or bookstore (amazingly we had more than one queer bookstore in Toronto in 1992), I came face to face with a barrage of safe-sex posters and safe-sex takeaway kits – a constant reminder that the sex I wanted was dangerous.

*** *The Flintstones* – 1994 ***

The B-52s still had enough cultural cachet to get hired as the house band in the 1994 *The Flintstones* live-action film. I hope they got a killer pay cheque because I think it's the biggest misstep in their career. Nobody came out of *The Flintstones* looking good, but it's the Bs, performing as The BC-52s, who suffered the most reputationally.

Admittedly, the carrot of being in a tentpole Hollywood film and a promotional video with Halle Berry, John Goodman, Kyle MacLachlan, Rick Moranis, Rosie O'Donnell, Elizabeth Perkins, and a quick cameo by Elizabeth Taylor is a pretty tempting one. I believe that this project helped cement the B-52s' later career status as a cartoon version of their former selves.

I can't really blame the band. Beyond the pay cheque, *The Flintstones* was a cultural phenomenon for those of us who grew up with the TV show. It was funny, irreverent, and full of great music and songs; being part of *The Flintstones* history would have been kind of irresistible. It didn't do a lot for their credibility as a serious rock band, but was that what the Bs were after all those years? Maybe it was the perfect move.

Keith is kind of hiding under his shag Beatle wig in the 'Meet the Flintstones' video, but Kate and Fred seem to be having a pretty gay old time. So, who am I to judge? Maybe having fun and making some cash is the ultimate win. Ironically, 'Meet the Flintstones' charted higher than 'Rock Lobster' ever did!

After *Good Stuff* and *The Flintstones*, things started to get better for queer people.

Antiretroviral drugs became more widely available in developed countries in the 1990s, and HIV no longer meant an immediate death sentence. The fight for marriage equality and partner benefits was gaining traction and would eventually become successful with the first gay marriage in Canada in 2003. The tireless efforts of researchers and scientists have resulted in PrEP (Pre-Exposure Prophylaxis) – a daily blue pill that's still prohibitively expensive for many – to help stop the spread of HIV.

After k.d. lang's seismic announcement that she was gay in 1992, there were finally out queers visible in music and pop culture. Ani DiFranco, Pansy Division, Melissa Etheridge, Indigo Girls, and any number of Riot Grrrl bands and members, to name a few. The B-52s pioneered queer visibility in popular music and changed the cultural landscape; maybe it was time for them to peace out for a bit. And they did. Probably for the best as the Bs were never going to fit in during the age of grunge. Imagine the B-52s in flannel?

To close out the 1990s, the Bs recorded a couple of tracks for the career retrospective release of *Time Capsule: Songs for a Future Generation* in 1998: 'Debbie' and 'Hallucinating Pluto' with Cindy back in the fold. The title of the collection seemed to suggest a farewell – a time capsule for a career that was now over. Strangely, the band got back together with Nile Rodgers in 2004 to record a Beatles cover for a Buick commercial. The B-52s did 'Paperback Writer'. Really.

*** *Funplex* – 2008 ***

You can't keep a good band down! The B-52s made fans wait fifteen years after *Good Stuff* for a new album, but we got one – *Funplex* was released 24 March 2008. The band were without a label and funded the recording sessions themselves. They hired producer Steve Osborne, who had worked with New Order and Happy Mondays, amongst many others. Osborne proved a great fit for the Bs.

Funplex is the most guitar-driven record in the band's catalogue after their first two albums, and it suits them. It's unlikely *Funplex* converted too many new fans to the radical queer joy of the B-52s, but it sure satisfied those of us who were still paying attention. The B-52s were having fun again! A video for the title track with dancing goth kids and security guards and another appearance by RuPaul, out of drag, helped push *Funplex* to number eleven on the Billboard 200 albums chart – the second highest-charting album of their career after *Cosmic Thing*.

A new album is a great way to keep touring interesting for a band that's been around a while, and this was true for the B-52s. Keith told *Rolling Stone* in advance of the release of *Funplex*: 'We thought, we're gonna keep [touring], we're gonna need some new songs for the show, we need to put a new album out there.'[5]

Is *Funplex* their best? No. But I love that they decided to make an album as a foursome again, give life to their touring show, and, most of all, erase *Good Stuff* and *The Flintstones* as their final recorded work together.

I got to see the band live again in the wake of *Funplex* – the first time for me since the early 1990s. By chance, they were playing the Hard Rock Cafe in Las Vegas a few days before I was meant to be in Sin City for a work trip. I couldn't pass up the chance to see one of my favourite bands again. Similar to that long-ago show at the Superstars club in Mississauga, I was worried that if I didn't go, I wouldn't get the chance again. I amended my travel plans to get to Vegas a few days early to catch the show. (Side note: NEVER spend more time than you have to in Vegas; seeing the Bs was a treat but I wanted to kill myself by the end of my trip.)

It was 12 June 2012, and after a few beers and wandering around the Hard Rock, I befriended two local gay guys in the crowd as we milled about and waited for the band to start. These two fellow travellers shared a joint with me, and it felt great to have a couple of new friends – my first B-52s show as an out queer, with a couple of my new gay pals. Heaven. Or so I thought. Just before the show was about to start, I looked around me hoping to find more of my queer tribe, but what I mostly saw were overweight and balding men in their forties and fifties. I realized in that moment that the B-52s had become a nostalgia act. Everyone's favourite kooks. Worse . . . a Vegas act. I focused on the band who were great and my new friends (also great) and managed to shake Keith's hand at the end of the show – finally, skin-to-skin contact with my earliest crush! It was like David (me) touching the hand of God (Keith) but in the Hard Rock Cafe in Vegas instead of the Sistine Chapel.

Notes

1 https://www.rollingstone.com/feature/love-shacks-rock-lobsters-and-nude-parties-the-b-52s-in-their-own-words-627925/

2 https://www.npr.org/2022/06/10/1104158276/julee-cruise-obituary-twin-peaks-david-lynch-b52s

3 https://ew.com/article/1992/06/26/good-stuff/

4 https://www.hiv.gov/hiv-basics/overview/history/hiv-and-aids-timeline#year-1992

5 https://www.rollingstone.com/music/music-news/first-b-52s-album-in-sixteen-years-loud-sexy-rock-roll-pumped-up-to-hot-pink-100334/

Conclusion

Nostalgia is a funny thing. And a dangerous one. There's something in particular about the nostalgia many people with kids hold on to – like their time as teenagers and college students was the best time of their lives. Reminiscing about a time before kids, mortgages, and careers took over every waking moment. On the opposite end of the spectrum, queer people must keep looking forward – to imagine brighter futures and queer utopias. Looking ahead to a time when being queer isn't a crime or despised.

Straight people, especially straight white people, are born into their utopia with a system and structure that centres them. Like the B-52s did with *Cosmic Thing*, queer people need to fight for our space, to constantly reinvent ourselves, throw out everything that came before, and start again. Every day. Queers grow up in a homophobic world, no matter what decade we are born in, and it's our duty to constantly look forward and imagine a brighter future for ourselves and for those who follow behind us.

I think it's that kind of nostalgia that keeps the B-52s locked in a weird limbo. The band is still out there touring, and they're delivering what the majority of the audience wants to see: crazy hair, 'Rock Lobster' and 'Love Shack'. Attendees of shows seem more interested in singing along and hearing their own voice, rather than witness an artistic act.

The B-52s are not alone out there. I see it more often than I'd like to. I was excited to see Tears for Fears when they were touring their excellent late career record, *The Tipping Point*. The band sounded incredible, and their new album was exquisite. They busted their ass to showcase their new material and almost no one in the audience cared. All the crowd seemed to want was to shout along to 'Everybody Wants to Rule the World' and then go back to their absurdly expensive beers and chat until another hit song from the 1980s came along. It's fine to want to hear the hits, but let's leave some room to be surprised.

Without fail, almost every queer person I told that I was writing this book responded with a squeal and a declaration of love for the B-52s. They would elaborate on how important the Bs were in helping them understand their own queerness, their colourfulness, and yes, their campiness. Just like me. Almost everyone else I told exclaimed 'cool, "Rock Lobster"!' The difference may not seem like much, but to me, it demonstrates everything about how queer people experience the world.

One of my oldest friends, another lifelong B-52s fan, is now a college professor in the US-Midwest. Talking about this book, we reminisced about listening to the Bs' first two records when we were teenagers. We talked about how I recognized something familiar in the B-52s but that their otherness sailed completely over his head – they were just a wacky band to him. We simply didn't have the language to talk about their queerness. That's how silencing works. If queerness is never acknowledged by the mainstream, it doesn't exist.

That silencing is confirmed to a degree by Keith, who told T. Cole Rachel, writing for *Pitchfork*: 'Not until 1992 did someone ask us about being gay'. It's amazing to think that no journalist asked the B-52s about their sexual identity until thirteen years after the band's debut. However, rock and roll press was still made up of almost exclusively white men, writing about white rock stars in the 1980s and 1990s, and most of them, like my friend the college professor, wouldn't have even thought to ask the question. Nor, I suspect, would they want to know the answer.[1]

Comedians have moved on from AIDS jokes; however, we now have the Dave Chapelles of the world punching down on trans folks. History repeating itself. This is not progress. The conservatives are still trying to find new ways to keep queers down and to keep us quiet. Book bans are a classic tactic used by repressive regimes throughout history and, incredibly, are being utilized again today. On top of book bans, many American states are now putting forward all manner of anti-drag and anti-trans legislation. In fact, more anti-LGBTQ bills were introduced in 2023 than in any other year in the history of the United States. Can I still say 'gay' in Florida?[2]

The manufactured furore over trans and non-binary people is just the latest tactic to rile up the right-wing voter base. Much like Tipper Gore's Parents Music Resource Center, Anita pie-in-the-face Bryant's bigotry, and the Mapplethorpe controversy – it's a blatant attempt to gain more power at the expense of an at-risk population. Politicians can keep introducing bills and they can keep trying to squash queer people, but like the B-52s did with *Cosmic Thing*, queers will reinvent, regroup, and find new ways to fight back. We will not go back into the closet. We will *walk in ecstasy*.

When I did finally come out of the closet and started heading out to my first gay bars, the B-52s was not what I heard over the sound systems. It was Diva city. A bunch of screaming women on top of overproduced dance beats. Where were the gays? Our actual foremothers and forefathers – our *forequeers*. I wanted to hear the bands I knew were queer, or at least had queer leanings and hints of otherness: the Smiths, R.E.M., Indigo Girls, k.d. lang, and yes, the B-52s. Sadly, that bar didn't exist in the early 1990s. It still doesn't. Maybe I just need to open my own damn bar and welcome the freaks, the weirdos, and those of us who have always felt 'other', even in our own gay community.

The B-52s aren't always considered as 'cool' as their contemporaries, like Blondie, The Ramones, the Go-Go's, and Talking Heads. All of those bands are defunct or took long breaks after their peak success. Maybe staying together and working out your differences is the coolest thing of all. The B-52s is one of those bands that has survived. Longevity for any band is a tricky proposition, but I think it's the band's approach to songwriting and, more importantly, sharing the benefits of songwriting – royalties and income – that is the key. Kate explains: 'Most of the songs were written by jamming together and we decided right away to split everything equally no matter what. No one wanted to fight over which song they wrote.' That's what friends do. That's what queers do.[3]

The split of royalties has brought down many, many bands, and it's the few, like Athens siblings R.E.M. and Irish behemoths U2, that made a similar decision to share songwriting credits. Both of those bands outlasted their contemporaries by years, even decades.

The B-52s still haven't asked me to join them; however, I did finally find *others like me*. Queers of all kinds who make art and music and buck traditional family and relationship models. I was even lucky enough to be invited to a recording studio and be part of a group of queer artists making music in the months before the COVID pandemic. *The Untitled Carolyn Taylor Project* felt akin to the B-52s' style of music making – improvising, jamming, singing, chanting, switching instruments, and then creating songs from the best bits caught on tape. A group of us even performed as a 'cat choir' for one of the tracks – the B-52s would undoubtedly be proud of us.

When the COVID pandemic struck, I was finally given time in my adult life to zone out and get bored. My partner and I would spend lazy days listening to my favourite records, the B-52s included. That time allowed me to rethink my relationship with the band and the Bs' position in popular music, planting the seeds for this analysis. I also used the time to finish my *first* book, *The Vinyl Diaries*, about two of my favourite things: my record collection and queer sex. Time and boredom worked for me in the creative process, much like it did for the B-52s.

I still don't have a real job. I'm an official member of the 'Deadbeat Club' and I've never been happier. It took me almost as long as the B-52s' storied career, but I'm finally confident in my own queerness. I still feel othered from the mainstream fairly often – the difference now is how grateful I am for it, in no small part thanks to the B-52s' example. They always demonstrated that to be of the other was cool. I still have *The B-52's*, *Wild Planet*, and *Party Mix!* album covers framed and up on my wall; they show the world who I am, where I came from. I like to think the Bs are my candy-coloured gay godparents watching over me.

When I put on my wig to perform in the Dolly Parton tribute choir (The Tennessee Mountain Homos) once a year, I think of my friends in the B-52s who showed me putting on a wig and playing dress-up wasn't just fun, it was queer. It took me over forty years to embrace that lesson, but with my wig, my false eyelashes, and a touch of black eyeliner, I give it my all. I sing from my heart. Just like Cindy. Just like Fred. Just like Kate. I lead with my heart and let the rest follow.

When I asked Chris Frantz at the end of our conversation if there was anything else he'd like to add, he used the word 'otherworldly'. First to describe Cindy's and Kate's stellar harmonies, but then we both bandied the word back and forth. 'That's how I feel about them', he concluded.[4] I couldn't agree more with Frantz. Otherworldly. From another place.

Many like to think that the HIV/AIDS pandemic is over, but according to UNAIDS, there were 39.9 million people living with HIV in 2023. That's a lot of people. The HIV/AIDS fight is far from over. The introduction of PrEP is an amazing aid in the fight against HIV infections, but it's still too damned expensive for a lot of us in the developed world, let alone the populations in developing nations. Like the Bs suggested in 'Channel Z', if we want that to change, it's up to us – *don't let it rest on the president's desk.*[5]

I still don't think the B-52s get the credit they deserve as queer pioneers. Remember the B-52s however you must – as the current threesome, the original fivesome, or even the foursome appearing as the BC-52s in *The Flintstones*. Whichever version you choose to remember, never forget the radical queer act they performed by just being part of the pop culture conversation for more than forty-five years.

In the face of rising conservatism and the ongoing HIV/AIDS pandemic, maybe we need the B-52s and *Cosmic Thing* more than ever. Play the B-52s LOUD. Play them PROUD. Play them often and dance. The B-52s are living queer icons and we should all remember them that way.

Notes

1 https://www.tcolerachel.com/b-52s

2 https://www.rollingstone.com/culture/culture-features/worst-anti-lgbtq-states-america-trans-legislation-1234788961/

3 https://juicemagazine.com/home/the-b-52s-kate-pierson-talks-sci-fi-surf-culture-groovy-music-lazy-desert-and-thrift-store-chic/

4 Chris Frantz interview, Aug 22, 2024.

5 https://www.unaids.org/en/resources/fact-sheet